RIGA

THE CITY AT A GLANCE

Central Market
It took six million bricks and 2,460 tonr iron to erect Europe's largest market in
See p080

National Opera
After a fire in 1882, the opera was rebuilt in a classical style. It marked its post-Soviet autonomy with an extensive renovation.
Aspazijas bulvāris 3, T 6707 3715

St Peter's Church
The 13th-century structure was wooden, but this Lutheran church now features a 123m metal steeple, which offers heavenly views.
Skārņu iela 19, T 6718 1430

National Library of Latvia
Dubbed the 'Castle of Light', Gunārs Birkerts' spectacular building resembles a forest of skyscrapers silhouetted against a mountain.
See p057

Nativity of Christ Cathedral
Its yellow brickwork and gilded domes make this 1884 neo-Byzantine church unmissable. The Soviets turned it into a raucous café, The God's Ear. It is now back in God's hands.
Brīvības bulvāris 23, T 6721 1207

St Jacob's Church
Of the Old Town's medieval churches, this Roman Catholic one is the smallest, with the slimmest tower and most authentic belfry.
Jēkaba iela 9

Z Towers
Raising Riga's skyline and set to top out in 2015, the 30-storey residential towers by city firm NRJA are circular with saw-tooth edges.
Daugavgrīvas iela

INTRODUCTION

THE CHANGING FACE OF THE URBAN SCENE

Despite half a century of Soviet occupation until independence in 1991 – a period when Riga stood still, culturally – Latvians remain positive, proud of any global attention. Indeed, initially the largest city in the Baltics seemed as if it were simply the quintessential Eurovision Song Contest destination, but its embrace of anything-goes tourism has given way to a maturity that accompanied entry into the EU in 2004, and the sobering effect of the economic crisis.

There is no need for razzmatazz to attract visitors. Riga's stock of art nouveau (see p027) and wooden architecture is some of the best in the world – and the USSR did at least leave behind some fine postwar modernism. With such a dowry, the city's architects and designers have become masters of renovation, and hotels and restaurants colonise historic properties dating back to the Middle Ages. Urban rebirth began with the modernisation of the airport and the unveiling of a 21st-century landmark, the National Library of Latvia (see p057). As the cash dried up, the focus shifted to civic spaces, best seen in the cultural quarter, Spīķeri (see p030).

After adopting all the benefits and drawbacks of Westernisation, Riga is unearthing its own identity, through 'new Latvian cuisine', eco-manufacturing and a fashion scene that encompasses Nordic minimalism and Slavic kitsch. This journey and ambition won the city the recognition it deserved when it was annointed Capital of Culture for 2014, as it finally placed its flag on the European map.

ESSENTIAL INFO

FACTS, FIGURES AND USEFUL ADDRESSES

TOURIST OFFICE

Rātslaukums 6
T 6703 7900
www.latvia.travel

TRANSPORT

Airport transfer to city centre
Bus no 22 departs every 10 to 30 minutes from approximately 6am to 12am. The journey takes 30 minutes and costs €1

Car hire
Avis
T 6722 5876

Taxi
Baltic Taxi
T 2000 8500

Travel card
An e-talons ticket covers bus and tram travel for 24 hours (€2.50) or 72 hours (€7)
www.rigassatiksme.lv

EMERGENCY SERVICES

Ambulance
T 03

Fire
T 01

Police
T 02

24-hour pharmacy
Rīgas Vecpilsētas Aptieka
Vaļņu iela 20
T 6721 3340

EMBASSIES

British Embassy
Jura Alunāna iela 5
T 6777 4700
www.gov.uk/government/world/latvia

US Embassy
Samnera Velsa iela
T 6710 7000
riga.usembassy.gov

POSTAL SERVICES

Post office
Stacijas laukums 2
T 6707 3900
www.pasts.lv

Shipping
UPS
Kārļa Ulmaņa gatve 2
T 6780 5650

BOOKS

Architectural Guide Riga
by Jānis Krastiņš (DOM)

The Dogs of Riga
by Henning Mankell (Vintage)

WEBSITES

Architecture
www.archmuseum.lv

Art/Culture
www.kulturasapvieniba.riga.lv

Newspaper
www.latviansonline.com

EVENTS

Cēsis Art Festival
www.cesufestivals.lv

Survival Kit
www.survivalkit.lv

COST OF LIVING

Taxi from Riga International Airport to city centre
€15

Cappuccino
€3

Packet of cigarettes
€3.50

Daily newspaper
€1.25

Bottle of champagne
€60

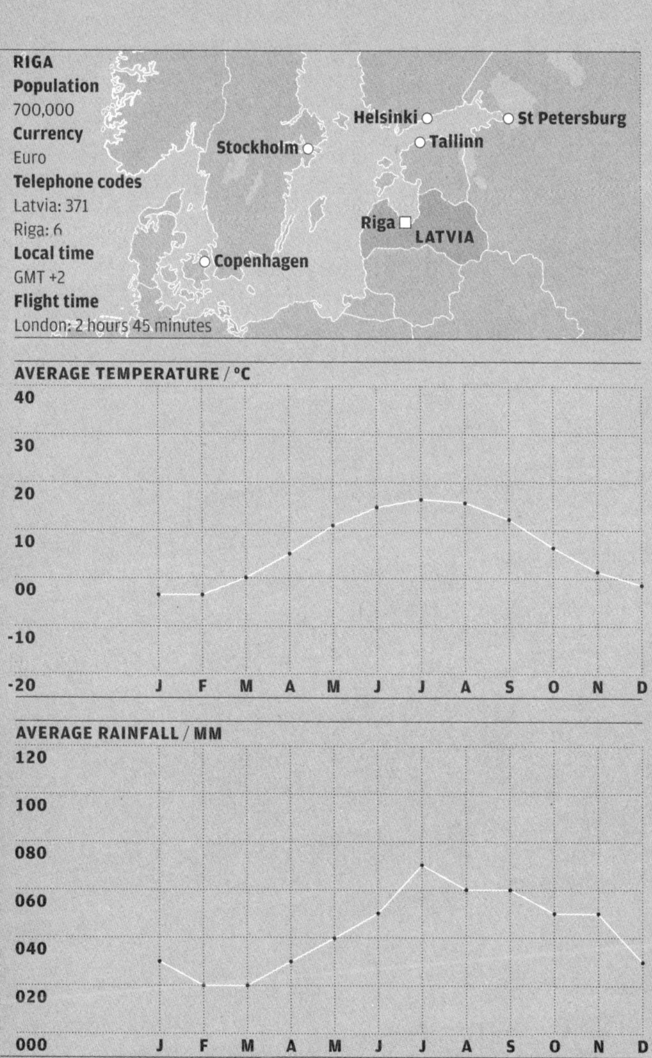
RIGA
Population
700,000
Currency
Euro
Telephone codes
Latvia: 371
Riga: 6
Local time
GMT +2
Flight time
London: 2 hours 45 minutes
Helsinki
St Petersburg
Tallinn
Stockholm
Riga
LATVIA
Copenhagen
AVERAGE TEMPERATURE / °C
40
30
20
10
00
-10
-20
J F M A M J J A S O N D
AVERAGE RAINFALL / MM
120
100
080
060
040
020
000
J F M A M J J A S O N D

NEIGHBOURHOODS

THE AREAS YOU NEED TO KNOW AND WHY

To help you navigate the city, we've chosen the most interesting districts (see below and the map inside the back cover) and colour-coded our featured venues, according to their location; those venues that are outside these areas are not coloured.

ĀGENSKALNS
This leafy working-class neighbourhood set on the west bank of the Daugava was mostly built between 1868 and 1911, and its narrow, cobblestoned streets are lined with wooden houses and art nouveau architecture. A flood of boho creatives has moved in recently in search of some peace, quiet and a sense of provincial community just five minutes' drive from the city centre.

ĶĪPSALA
A decade or so ago, this island was an overgrown 'hood of rundown wooden homes and fishermen's shacks. However, many have since been modernised and, due to the conversion of a plaster factory into lofts and Fabrikas Restorāns (see p048), the arrival of the Swedbank HQ (see p013) and the expansion of the Technical University campus, this enclave is becoming almost unrecognisable. Yet there's still history here, most notably in the Žanis Lipke Memorial (see p026).

MASKAVAS
Situated along the road to the Russian capital is the 'Moscow' district. The Jewish ghetto was established here in 1941, and a white concrete memorial was unveiled on Gogoļa iela in 2007: *Rescuer of the Jews* was created by Latvian artist Elina Lazdiņa and has been inscribed with the names of 270 Rigans who aided the Jews during the Holocaust. Also worth seeing in Maskavas is the Academy of Sciences (see p015).

CENTRS
Riga's compact city centre is separated from the Old Town (Vecrīga) by Pilsētas canal, which winds through a series of parks and gardens. Roughly a third of the buildings here were constructed in an art nouveau style (see p027), mainly between 1896 and 1913. Centrs is where you'll find two of Riga's best dining spots, Bergs (see p034) and Vincents (see p052).

VECRĪGA
The largely traffic-free cobbled streets of Riga's historic core are a delight to amble through as they offer up squares packed with outdoor cafés and a diverse mix of fascinating buildings – find out more at the medieval Three Brothers, home to the Latvian Museum of Architecture (Mazā Pils iela 19, T 6722 0779). The concentration in Vecrīga of bars and clubs, and upscale restaurants and hotels – such as Neiburgs (see p017) and Dome (see p020) – is such that some never leave, which is a shame.

ANDREJSALA
Cut off by the railway, this semi-derelict industrial port area became popular with skate kids, artists and designers, who converted its abandoned warehouses into studios, workshops and galleries in an initial wave of reclamation, but the scene has since moved on. These days, the reason to visit is the row of restaurant/bars along the gentrified waterfront, two of them (see p024) designed by architect Zane Tetere.

LANDMARKS

THE SHAPE OF THE CITY SKYLINE

Ride the lift up to the 72m-high observation platform in St Peter's Church (Skārņu iela 19, T 6718 1430) or linger over a cocktail in the Skyline Bar (see p050) at the summit of Radisson Blu Hotel Latvija (Elizabetes iela 55, T 6777 2222), and you will discover that Riga is a low-rise city with few prominent features. This is largely a result of the Soviet government's focus on industrial production and prefabricated housing, although it did contribute some notable landmarks: the Academy of Sciences (see p015), the Museum of the Occupation (Strēlnieku laukums 1) and the distant TV Tower (see p014), which soars above the largest island in the Daugava. Earlier 20th-century structures of note include the Central Market (see p080), whose scale is strangely at odds with the quaintness of the surrounding streets, and the Freedom Monument (see p012).

Riga's early noughties construction boom resulted in significant buildings and dilapidated areas gaining a new a lease of life, but several ambitious, high-profile projects have fallen victim to the global downturn, including OMA/Rem Koolhaas' conversion of an Andrejsala power station into an art space. One that did survive is the residential high-rise Z Towers, not far from the equally shiny Swedbank HQ (see p013). Also underway is a full-scale renovation of the National Museum of Art (Krišjāņa Valdemāra iela 10a), a massive neoclassical building from 1905 that will reopen in 2016. *For full addresses, see Resources.*

Vanšu Tilts

This striking cable-stayed concrete bridge, which has a 109m-tall concrete pylon at its centre, was built during the Soviet era and inaugurated in 1981. It was originally called Gorky Tilts in honour of the Russian novelist (its modern name simply means 'cable bridge'), and it carries the airport road 595m over the Daugava to the centre of Riga. Vanšu remained the newest of four bridges spanning the river, before the fifth, Dienvidu Tilts (which translates as 'southern bridge'), was completed in late 2008, with the specific intention of reducing congestion. Designed by a trio of practices – Tiltprojekts, St Petersburg Design Institute and Arhitektonika – the Dienvidu is a six-lane, 803m overpass, founded on 10 piers. It has six pylons, as well as screens that have been erected in order to minimise traffic noise.

Freedom Monument

Marking the boundary between the Old Town and the city centre, this 42m-high monument, affectionately dubbed 'Milda' by locals, was designed by the Latvian sculptor Kārlis Zāle and finished in 1935 to celebrate the 17th anniversary of the country's declaration of independence. Funded by public donations, it consists of a granite column topped by a statue of a woman holding three golden stars that represent Latvia's provinces – Kurzeme, Vidzeme and Latgale. The column's base is carved with reliefs of soldiers, workers and families, often surrounded by red and white flowers (the colours of the national flag). This wasn't always the case, however. During Soviet times, laying flowers here was banned and a statue of Lenin (now dismantled) was erected nearby.
Brīvības bulvāris

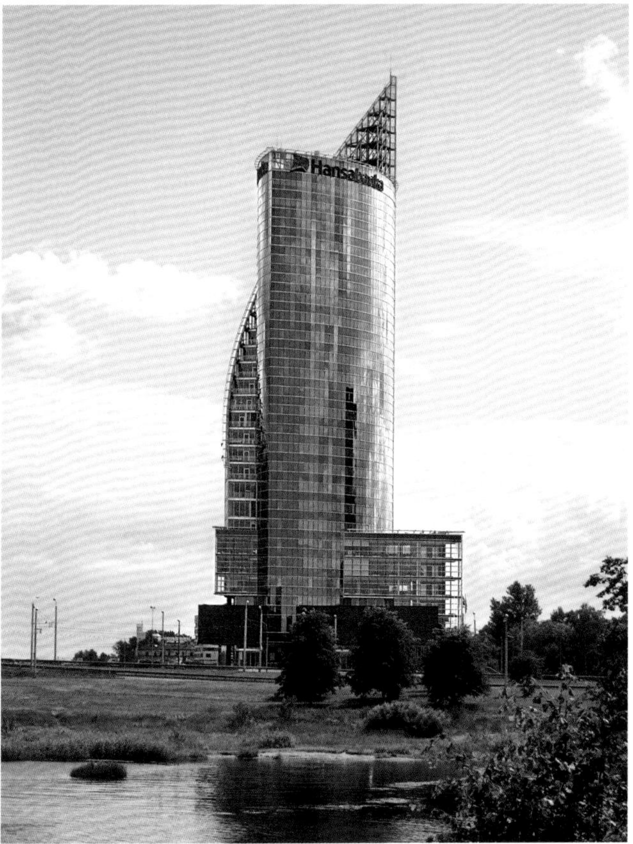

Swedbank Headquarters

The first skyscraper to be built in newly independent Latvia, this 121m tower, just over the Vanšu Tilts (see p010), is the HQ of Swedbank (previously Hansabanka). Designed by Viktors Valgums of Zenico Projekts and Alvis Zlaugotnis of Tectum, it was completed in 2004 as part of a grand plan for the left bank of the Daugava. The building's glazed facade is fully transparent from certain angles, while the sail-like fin echoes the waterside location. There is a café on the 25th floor, but you'll have to befriend an employee if you want to catch the sweeping views. It held the title of the tallest building in Riga for a decade, but is soon to be overshadowed by the 130m Z Towers nearby on Daugavgrīvas iela, a pair of conjoined cylinders conceived by NRJA, and due for completion in 2015.
Balasta dambis 1a, www.swedbank.lv

TV Tower

The slightly wild Zaķusala (Rabbit Island) is a 30-minute stroll from the Old Town and is reached by walking underneath the concrete Salu Tilts ('island bridge'). Rising from one end of it like a red-and-yellow Eiffel Tower is this component of Riga's television and radio broadcasting system. Completed in 1989, the TV Tower is the tallest structure in the Baltic states at 368m. Designed by Kim Nikuradze, Viktor Savchenko and Nikolaj Sergijevskiy, the tower is supported by three slanting legs, two of which accommodate the high-speed elevators that transport visitors to the observation floor from where they can enjoy a spectacular 360-degree panorama. The interior is also likely to raise a smile, with an aesthetic that is part Soviet-era control centre, part *Star Trek* set.
Zaķusalas krastmala 1, www.tvtornis.lv

Academy of Sciences

Rigans are not keen on this skyscraper, designed by Russian architect Lev Rudnev, and it's not hard to understand why, once you learn it was a gift from the Soviets, intended to mark the outer reaches of Stalin's empire. This reminder of the bad days is tucked away in the shabby Moscow quarter behind the station, and is largely ignored. Its 108m facade is decorated with hammers and sickles and, at the time of its completion in 1956, it was one of the world's highest reinforced concrete buildings. Today, it doubles as the home of the Academy of Sciences and holds an archive of Latvian folk tales and songs. The curator will whisk you up in the lift to the 17th floor, where several flights of stairs stand between you and a balcony affording stunning alfresco views.
Akadēmijas laukums 1, T 6722 5361

HOTELS

WHERE TO STAY AND WHICH ROOMS TO BOOK

For a city of such modest size, Riga has plenty of hotels, although most have yet to move beyond floral bedspreads and chintz: many tout themselves as 'boutique', 'minimalist' or 'Scandinavian', and are actually anything but. One place that does get it right, however, is Hotel Bergs (see p018), an upmarket retreat in a lovely enclave. If you'd prefer to be based right in the heart of the art nouveau district, the Valdemārs (Krišjāņa Valdemāra iela 23, T 6733 4462) is a hotel and apartment complex located in a turn-of-the-century building, whereas the modern, 11-storey Albert Hotel (Dzirnavu iela 33, T 6733 1717) has a roof lounge (see p043) with fine vistas.

Two recent openings are wholly contemporary but beautifully housed inside historical properties. The flamboyant facade of the 1903 Neiburgs (opposite) was designed by Wilhelm Bockslaff and features the chiselled visage of its namesake financier. The Dome (see p020) is older still – even if you're not staying, its terrace bar and restaurant is within touching distance of the cathedral bells. Of the more venerable establishments, the Grand Palace Hotel (see p022) remains the city's most elegant address, and the Europa Royale (Krišjāņa Barona iela 12, T 6707 9444), finished in 1876, had a colourful past before being turned into a hotel in 2006. Rooms are adorned with rich colours, ornate fabrics and parquet flooring, and a 1930s Venetian chandelier illuminates the restaurant.

For full addresses and room rates, see Resources.

Hotel Neiburgs

One of the city's most ornate art nouveau buildings, the Neiburgs was renovated with the help of designer Iveta Cibule. The oak parquet floors, painted ceilings, stucco detailing and Bohemia cast-iron radiators are now complemented by contemporary pieces, as in the library (above), while an original tile pattern has been repeated in headboard murals, and walls are decorated with graphic art. Of the 55 residential-style suites, the best are in the eaves, due to superb panoramas. Indulge in the spa's signature treatment, a buckwheat honey wrap, before dinner in the restaurant, once a beer hall for the nomenklatura, which serves up Tomass Godiņš' Gallic-influenced Latvian cuisine below Ron Gilad's spider-like 'Dear Ingo' chandelier. *Jauniela 25-27, T 6711 5522, www.neiburgs.com*

Hotel Bergs

This boutique property, created by the Rigan architect Zaiga Gaile with Andrejs Andersons, displays paintings by Latvian old masters and 120 modern works by Ilmārs Blumbergs, who also designed the courtyard fountain. There are 38 apartment-style rooms, which all have oak floors and period fireplaces – our favourite is the Penthouse (pictured).
Elizabetes iela 83-85, T 6777 0900

Dome Hotel

In his delicate conversion of this 17th-century home, architect Reinis Liepins has blended historical substance with custom-made furniture, as on the rickety wooden staircase (opposite). The 15 rooms are highly individual – the Deluxe Suite 201 (above), for instance, is enhanced by ceiling, coving and wall paintings from the turn of the 19th century and 'Macchina della Luce' chandeliers by Catellani & Smith. The spa synthesises oriental and Baltic traditions and incorporates marine-based treatments; there's also a hammam and sauna. In-house restaurant Le Dome specialises in fish, and in summer has two terraces, one overlooking a vertical garden in the inner courtyard, and the other on the fifth floor, with a barbecue grill.
Miesnieku iela 4, T 6750 9010, www.domehotel.lv

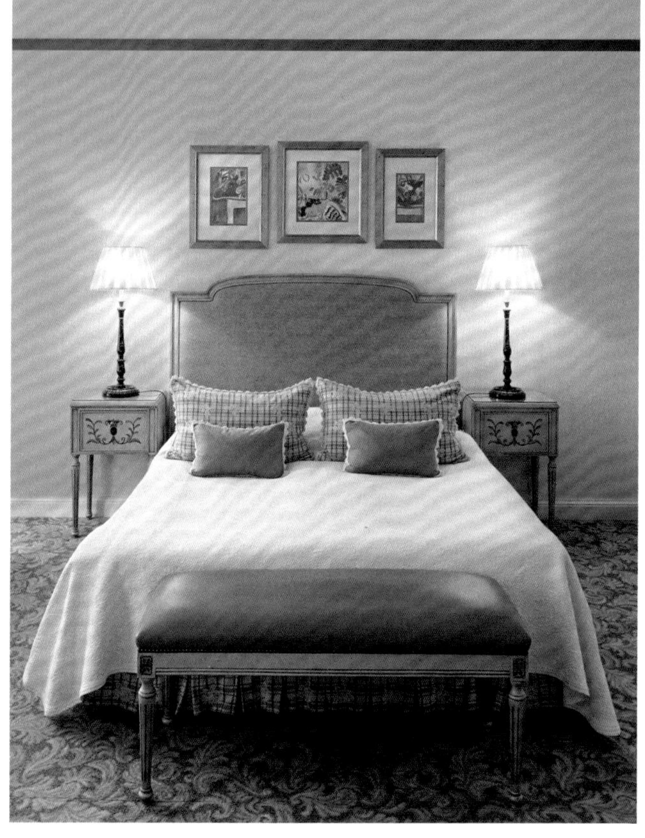

Grand Palace Hotel

Constructed on the foundations of a 15th-century fortress in 1877, the former Central Bank of Latvia is tucked away on a cobbled street near the castle and Three Brothers: medieval stone dwellings that now house the Museum of Architecture (T 6722 0779). The building was converted into a hotel in 2000, and blends Russian and European interior influences to generate a stately elegance. The Grand Palace is a favourite of diplomats and dignitaries, who gather over drinks in the Pils Bar – which is adorned with hunting trophies – or take lunch in the restaurant and on its summer terrace. The Junior Suites, such as 303 (above), have plenty of space and walk-in closets. The basement sauna and steam room can be booked for private sessions.
Pils iela 12, T 6704 4000,
www.grandpalaceriga.com

Hotel Centra

Next to the pretty churches of St John and St Peter's (see p009), the contemporary-styled Centra has been open since 2000. Thanks to a mix of frequent renovations and a minimalist design, evidenced in the lobby (above), it has avoided becoming dated. Housed in an eclectic late 19th-century building, the 27 high-ceilinged rooms exhibit a safe palette of brown and white, the only frills being paintings by Latvian artists and giant TVs. Opt for one at the rear of the building as there are some lively clubs nearby; top-floor suites have views across the Old Town roofscape. The buffet breakfast and lunch at Café Olé in the vaults are popular with guests and locals alike. Centra's design-on-a-budget ethos draws a young, stylish crowd.
Audēju iela 1, T 6722 6441,
www.hotelcentra.lv

24 HOURS

SEE THE BEST OF THE CITY IN JUST ONE DAY

It doesn't take long to cover a lot of ground in Riga. Wake up with an espresso and country eggs at Žanna (opposite) and then take a stroll through Centrs to appreciate the Latvian adaptation of art nouveau (see p027), keeping your eyes skyward so as not to miss the splendid detailing. Highlights are the national romantic buildings by Aleksandrs Vanags (Krišjāņa Valdemāra iela 69) and Eižens Laube (Brīvības iela 37, 47 and 62). Also in this quarter is the Janis Rozentāls and Rūdolfs Blaumanis Memorial Museum (Alberta iela 12, T 6733 1641), which is dedicated to the work of two Latvian cultural giants. In the Old Town, Vecrīga, you'll find a staggering number of cultural venues. Art Museum Riga Bourse (Doma laukums 6, T 6722 3434), Museum of Decorative Arts and Design (Skārņu iela 10-20, T 6722 2235) and Arsenāls Exhibition Hall (Torņa iela 1, T 6735 7527) promote interesting shows, from classic Latvian works to contemporary photography and fashion.

End your day at the refined Vincents (see p052), which serves superb Baltic cuisine, or jump in a taxi (they're plentiful and cheap) up to Andrejsala to dine at stylish Koya (see p031) or Aqua Luna (Andrejostas iela 4, T 6765 0922) before heading to nearby club First Dacha (Andrejostas iela 4a, T 2654 0555) to get a groove on. Note that bouncers' interpretation of 'face control' can be an issue if you don't speak Latvian or Russian – best to befriend the locals.

For full addresses, see Resources.

10.00 Žanna Café

This corner premises opened in 2014 in a quiet neighbourhood, and quickly earned a reputation for its coffee – a scarlet La Marzocco espresso machine takes pride of place. The focus is firmly on the bean but, from the limited menu, breakfasts include poached eggs and porridge, homemade quiche and fresh pastries. Žanna is set in a 1930s functionalist building with original wood panelling and a curved concrete balcony above the entrance; and the walls, high ceiling and exposed pipes have been given a lime-green paint job. Watch the world go by from the windowsill benches, or huddle up to the giant radiators in the winter. The cosy space facilitates random encounters, especially as it's open until 10pm, serving bottled beers, wine and G&Ts, and attracts a friendly local crowd. *Tomsona iela 2, T 2700 2226*

12.00 Žanis Lipke Memorial

In a cul-de-sac on Ķīpsala is a black shed-like memorial to the docker Žanis Lipke, who saved the lives of more than 50 Jews in WWII by hiding them in a bunker in his backyard (his family still lives next door). Designed by Zaiga Gaile, it opened in 2011. A dark passage leads to a shaft connecting the three levels of the building. From the attic, visitors can peer down into a well symbolising the bunker, in its original 3m by 3m dimensions, that 'housed' up to 12 people; nine wooden bunks drop down from the walls. Above the pit is a *sukkah*, a symbolic Jewish shelter, with paintings by Kristaps Ģelzis. The ambience and personal artefacts make it an emotional experience. Open 12pm to 6pm (8pm on Thursdays). Closed Mondays, and Sundays in winter. *Mazais Balasta dambis 8, T 6720 2539, www.lipke.lv*

13.15 Art Nouveau District

Besides its sheer quantity of art nouveau architecture (about 800 buildings), Riga offers a uniquely Latvian variation on the style, blending fantastical elements with geometrical ornamentation. Many striking examples are on Alberta iela, including several by Mikhail Eisenstein, such as 2a (above) from 1906, which, along with its bas relief and elaborate rooftop, features a host of statues, and sphinxes guarding the entrance. Number 12, designed by Konstantīns Pēkšēns and Eižens Laube, has stylised reliefs of squirrels and pine cones, and was home to the painter Jānis Rozentāls and writer Rūdolfs Blaumanis. It houses a museum dedicated to them (see p024) that provides the chance to see a genuine 1903 art nouveau interior. The centrepiece is a spiral staircase with ceiling paintings said to be by Rozentāls.

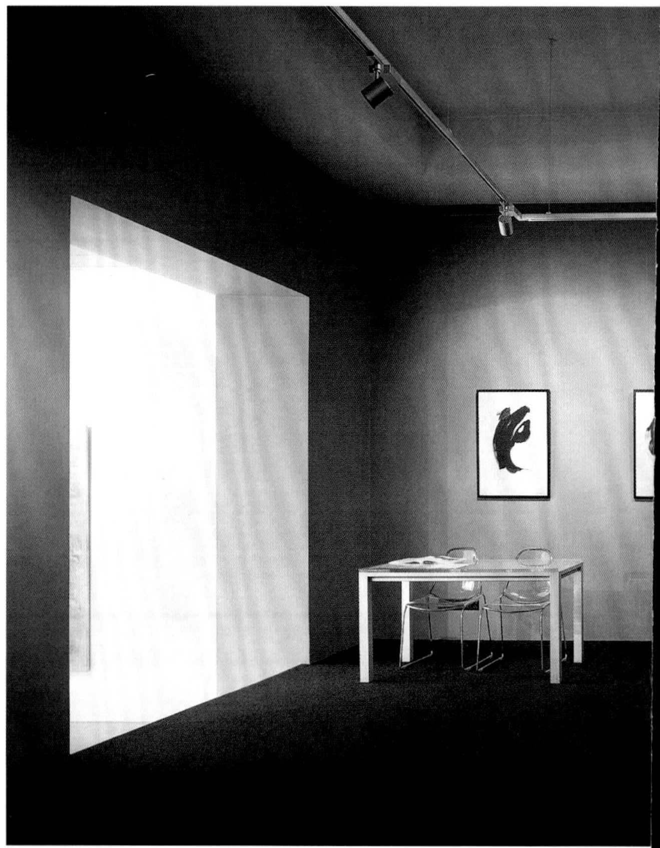

15.30 Māksla XO

Have lunch at the lovely Bistro Priedaine (T 6728 2122) before heading round the corner to one of the city's most important galleries, set on the ground floor of a 1930 functionalist building designed by Teodors Hermanovskis. Founder and curator Ilze Žeivate focuses on contemporary painting, graphic art, sculpture and photography, and represents big hitters such as Ieva Iltnere, Frančeska Kirke, Kristaps Ģelzis and Ilze Lībiete ('In The Shadow', above) in both solo exhibitions and annual group shows. Māksla also hosts retrospectives on Latvian masters from the early 20th century to the 1970s, and next-generation artists including Kaspars Podnieks, who represented Latvia in the 2013 Venice Biennale. The gallery closes on Sundays. *Elizabetes iela 14, T 2948 2098, www.makslaxogalerija.lv*

16.30 Spīķeri

Built between 1864 and 1886, 13 red-brick shipping warehouses behind the railway station have been reconstituted into a landscaped cultural hub with a riverfront promenade. Come here for shows by the State Chamber Orchestra and the Latvian Radio Choir. Or view the conceptual pieces on display at Kim? ('What is art?'; T 6722 3321), a gallery that promotes monthly exhibitions – 'North by Northeast: The Deconstruction of the Pavilion' featured Krišs Salmanis' 'moving tree' installation (above) – as well as film screenings and musical performances (Tuesday, 12-8pm; Wednesday to Sunday, 12-6pm). Among the other ventures in Spīķeri are further art spaces, boutiques and the Desa & Co bistro (T 6721 6186), which flips organic venison and wild boar burgers.
Maskavas iela 4, www.spikeri.lv

20.00 Koya

In 2012, architect Zane Tetere of OpenAD repurposed a graffitied shack into a chic riverside destination. The major draw is the glass-walled terrace, bedecked with miniature trees, Harry Bertoia chairs and heaters for chilly evenings, a perfect spot to savour the day's oysters, as yachts and ferries glide past. Inside, the concrete, brickwork and garage-door shutters have been retained, the ceiling has been clad with recycled timber, the chandeliers are by metal artist Edgars Spridzāns and there's a vertical garden. Dine on creative European dishes such as sea trout tartare with caviar on toasted rye, or kohlrabi salad with sunflower-seed cream and smoked eel. At weekends, DJs play jazz, electronica, soul and hip hop until 1am.
Andrejostas iela 4, T 2775 7255, www.koyarestaurant.com

URBAN LIFE

CAFÉS, RESTAURANTS, BARS AND NIGHTCLUBS

Latvian cuisine is big on potatoes, meat and cabbage. If you want the full-on traditional experience, visit the Lido Recreation Centre (Krasta iela 76, T 6750 4420), an eaterie in a super-kitsch log cabin and windmill inside an amusement park. Dining out has come a long way since independence, and many of the city's top kitchens show ambition, variety and imagination. There are still few places that could compete globally, but the scene is looking up due to the arrival of establishments such as Bibliotēka No 1 (see p053). Here, and at the perennial favourites Bergs (see p034) and Vincents (see p052), the locally sourced ingredients and creative, well-executed cooking are fostering a fledgling culinary movement. Booking is not required at most restaurants, but do reserve a table at these.

Drinking, on the other hand, is one of Riga's strong suits. Every bar, café and lounge boasts a comprehensive selection of tipples. The nightlife is generally lively, although many places don't really get going until after midnight. If you would like to start the party earlier, order a Latvian mojito from one of the sullen waitresses in the Skyline Bar (see p050) and settle down to watch the sun set. Later on, Piens (see p044) and Kaņepes Culture Centre (Skolas iela 15, T 2940 4405) put on events and happenings within vintage, shabby-chic interiors every night of the week. Quintessential Riga, these are the spots where the city's creative class loosens up.

For full addresses, see Resources.

Garage Wine Bar

Grey concrete and stainless steel dominate the interior of this former 1930s garage, but vintage wooden tables, automobile paraphernalia and contemporary art and photography add warmth. The venue advertises itself as 'democratic', which in Latvia means fine home cooking at a reasonable price. There are soups, salads and a limited dinner menu, but the main draw is the generous platters of Spanish tapas and the well-edited wine list, all of which is available by the glass. Garage shares a large courtyard with Restaurant Bergs (see p034) and the Andalūzijas Suns pub (T 6728 8418). In summer, the three fill Bergs Bazaar with chatter from late afternoon (aperitif time is from 3pm until 6pm) well into the long evenings.
Elizabetes iela 83-85, T 2662 8833, www.vinabars.lv

Restaurant Bergs
Nauris Jakuško is one of the most exciting chefs in Riga and he updates Bergs' menu every fortnight, using seasonal produce including Baltic herring, buckwheat and lingonberry. Book in advance to try his delightfully presented five-course tasting menu (€65) that might feature red-deer tartare with grilled baby leeks, or scallops with caramelised chicory, mussel reduction and seaweed salad. The dark, monochrome interior, with a chequerboard floor, African woodcarvings and textiles, leather and woven furniture and a ceiling installation symbolising cabbages (Kristaps Bergs developed his bazaar here at the end of the 19th century on a vegetable patch outside the city walls) is cosy in winter. But when the sun's out, take advantage of a table on the veranda or the terrace overlooking the courtyard fountain.
Hotel Bergs, Elizabetes iela 83-85, T 6777 0957, www.hotelbergs.lv

Vilhelms Ķuze

For a glimpse of what Riga looked like before the Nazis and the Soviets occupied the city, visit this Viennese-style café. Named after the man who founded the chocolate and biscuit factory Staburadze in 1910, it looks much as it might have done in the 1930s, all black-and-white tiled flooring, upright piano and art deco furnishings. Despite offering plenty of intriguing menu options, such as 'hunter's salad', the café is very popular with Riga's ladies who lunch. And not necessarily for the actual lunch – rather the six kinds of hot chocolate, liqueur coffees, and even alcoholic tea (with cognac and honey). Take away a box of handmade truffles to indulge in later. Also recommended for chocoholics is Emils Gustavs (T 6722 8333) on Aspazijas bulvāris, near the opera.
Jēkaba iela 20-22, T 6732 2943, www.kuze.lv

Bufete Gauja

This tiny café is reminiscent of a late 1960s Soviet-era living room. There are graphic-print armchairs and triangular coffee tables; kitsch Eastern European portraits; locally made Gauja radios; old-school board games such as chess, Ludo and draughts; and shelves stacked with vintage magazines and vinyl, including the odd Elvis record. It makes for a retro-chic stop for a mid-afternoon sharpener, whether it's an espresso or shot of vodka. The drinks menu is cheap and extensive; try a Latvian beer like Tērvetes or the unpasteurised, sweet and acquired taste of Brenguļu. The bar is popular with an arty college set, and can be rowdy. There's a smaller Gauja inside alt-club Nabaklab (Zigfrīda Annas Meierovica bulvāris 12).
Tērbatas iela 56, T 6727 5662,
www.bufetegauja.lv

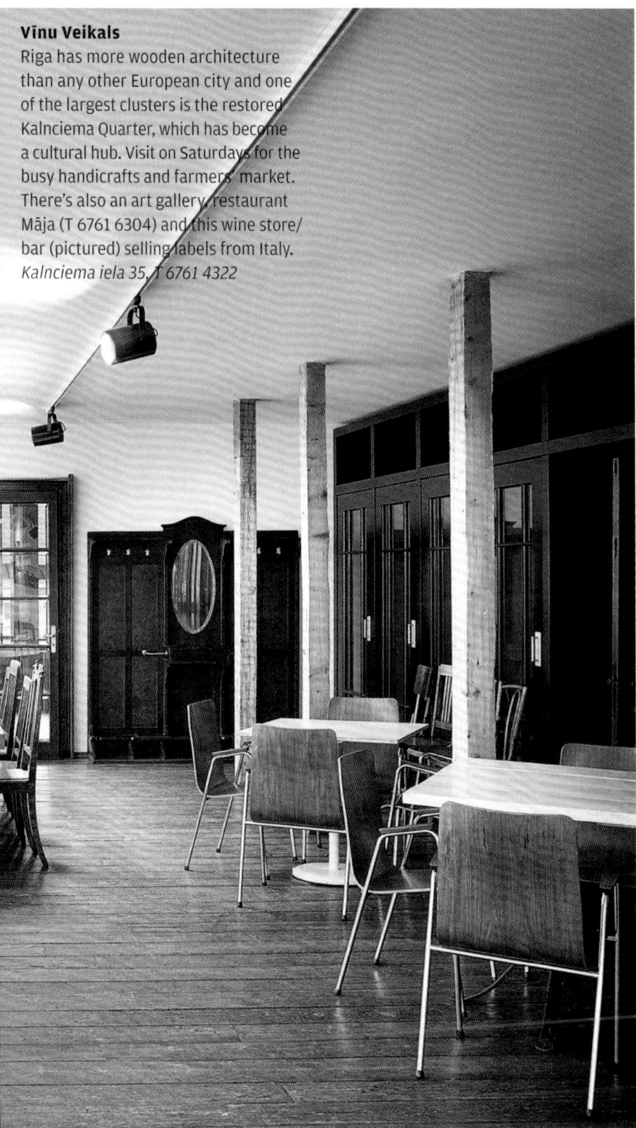

Vīnu Veikals

Riga has more wooden architecture than any other European city and one of the largest clusters is the restored Kalnciema Quarter, which has become a cultural hub. Visit on Saturdays for the busy handicrafts and farmers' market. There's also an art gallery, restaurant Māja (T 6761 6304) and this wine store/bar (pictured) selling labels from Italy.
Kalnciema iela 35, T 6761 4322

Black Magic Bar

Latvia's potent liqueur, Black Balsam (see p078), was created by Rigan pharmacist Abraham Kunze in 1752. A combination of more than 20 ingredients, including birch bud, linden blossom, valerian root, ginger, raspberry, bilberry, nutmeg and black peppercorn, it's brewed in oak barrels and served in myriad ways. You order it warm or cold, added to tea or coffee, or mixed with juice or even vodka. If the original brew is too strong, try the sweeter cream or blackcurrant version. It also appears in chocolates, cookies and desserts. All this and more will be explained in the Black Magic Bar's candlelit underground cellar at one of its nightly 'alchemy' shows. The demonstrations, most definitely aimed at tourists, are more than a touch cheesy, but after several Balsam-laced cocktails and nibbles, you probably won't care.
Kaļķu iela 10, T 6722 2877, www.blackmagic.lv

Galerija Istaba

Graphic designer and artist Linda Lūse opened Istaba, which means 'room', back in 2004 and it remains as distinctive as ever, thanks to the eclectic furnishings she sourced from secondhand markets and vintage shops. On the ground level is a gallery selling postcards of old Latvian posters, art and design magazines and books, cards, notebooks, matchboxes, T-shirts, jewellery and ceramics by local artists, such as Maruta Raude and Aivars Vilipsons. It also hosts regular exhibitions, as well as book launches, performances and concerts. The cosy mezzanine café, done out with mix-and-match wallpaper panels and an oddball aggregation of furniture, is where you will find Riga's artists, writers and actors animatedly discussing their most recent projects.
Krišjāņa Barona iela 31a, T 6728 1141

Star Lounge Bar

Albert Hotel is one of the best adaptations of Soviet modernism in Riga. The 10-storey prefab concrete block – a strangely cheery home for the 1970s Experimental Institute of Planning – was topped by a twisted glass-and-steel volume by local architects Arhis in 2005. Here, the Star Lounge Bar has views of Swedbank HQ (see p013), Vanšu Tilts (see p010) and several spires; in summer, bag a spot on the slightly scary cantilevered balcony. On cold nights, the Winter Delux (spiced rum, apple, honey, grenadine and lemon) might soothe the glare from the garish lighting and carpet, and there's a decent Sunday brunch buffet too. The hotel is named after Einstein, who struck up a literary friendship with Rigan scientist Rudolf Karklins.
Dzirnavu iela 33, T 6714 2749, www.alberthotel.lv

Piens

Zane Tetere paid homage to the 1930s in this conversion of a brewery into a 'sofa bar' with pastel blocks, retro objects and mismatched furniture. The café/cocktail lounge/club, the epicentre of a hip scene, is busy day and night (queues start from 10pm; Wednesdays are recommended) with exhibitions, screenings and gigs. The rear courtyard hosts boutique festivals.
Aristida Briāna iela 9a, T 6601 6300

Cabo Cafe

On the shores of Ķīšezers Lake, a little way out of town, Cabo has been developed from a windsurf shed into a laidback canteen/ bar. Head here late afternoon in summer, after an architour through Mežaparks (see p067), to join the designer sneakers and shades crowd and hip young families on the terrace for a sundowner, and perhaps a grilled trout from the BBQ. Beanbags and tables are also set up on the lawn, close to the water's edge. The more energetic can head to the watersports centre where there's a windsurfing school and board and boat rental, or join the ladies doing surfboard yoga; there's a swimming area nearby too. Also right on the lake is the lovely Ozo Golf Club (T 6739 4399), which has its fair share of water hazards.
Annas Sakses 19a/Roberta Feldmaņa iela 8, T 2863 9556, www.cabo.lv

Vīna Studija

Young architect Mārtiņš Pīlēns kickstarted his career with the accomplished interior of Vīna Studija (Wine Studio), which also has branches on Elizabetes iela (T 6728 3205) and in several malls in Riga and Liepāja. Pīlēns stripped back the space for an industrial feel, softened by plenty of pine. Spotlights and anglepoises showcase solo exhibitions by contemporary painters and photographers such as Aija Zariņa and Elita Patmalniece. There's a large glass wine cellar, a sociable bar area, an intimate restaurant and an adjoining store offering more than 800 labels from all over the world. The Mediterranean tapas is a perfect accompaniment to the grape; more substantial dishes include chestnut-apple cream soup with duck breast salad. *Stabu iela 30, T 6727 6010, www.vinastudija.lv*

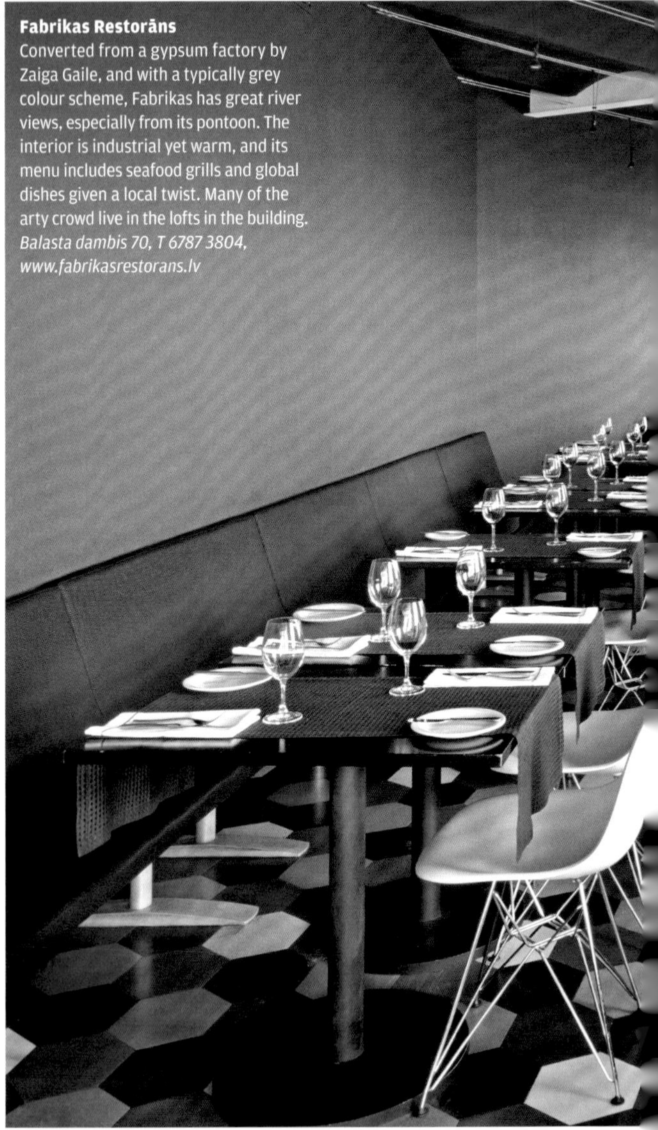

Fabrikas Restorāns
Converted from a gypsum factory by Zaiga Gaile, and with a typically grey colour scheme, Fabrikas has great river views, especially from its pontoon. The interior is industrial yet warm, and its menu includes seafood grills and global dishes given a local twist. Many of the arty crowd live in the lofts in the building.
Balasta dambis 70, T 6787 3804, www.fabrikasrestorans.lv

Skyline Bar

The 27-storey Radisson Blu (see p009) is among the tallest buildings in town. Take the glass lift to the 26th floor for one of the best views you'll get of the city with a drink in hand. This is where the beautiful and the monied come to chinwag over great cocktails; the list includes the warming Hot Winter in Latvia, made with, of course, the ubiquitous Black Balsam, blackcurrant juice, orange and cinnamon. The bar's floor-to-ceiling windows offer 360-degree vistas (there's even a stunning view from the toilets), making this a popular spot at sunset, so arrive early to snag one of the banquettes or leather swivel chairs. The frosty service is a little less inspiring, and be warned, stag parties often invade at the weekend, with all that entails.
Radisson Blu Hotel Latvija, Elizabetes iela 55, T 6777 2282, www.skylinebar.lv

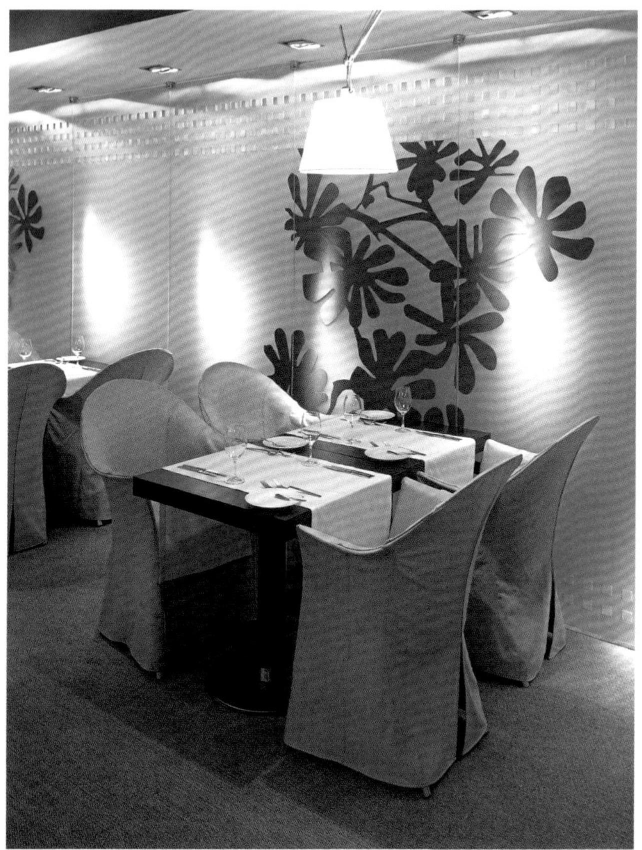

Vincents

This gastronomic hotspot opened in 1994, and is where all visiting celebrities and royals head for dinner. Owner and chef, Mārtiņš Rītiņš, is an advocate of the slow food movement and uses fresh, organic produce from Latvian farmers to create cutting-edge Baltic cuisine. Everything, down to the delicious bread rolls, is made from scratch, and the constantly changing menu is matched with wine pairings from the sophisticated cellar. The interior was redesigned in 2008 by Guna Eglīte and Zane Lāce to give the place a lighter, more contemporary feel; the bar's 'forest' of black poles and 'Lem' bar stools by Shin and Tomoko Azumi complement the warm ambience of the restaurant, whose subtly lit walls feature floral panels by Cappellini.
Elizabetes iela 19, T 6733 2830,
www.vincents.lv

Bibliotēka No 1

Before helping to launch Bibliotēka No 1 in 2011, young chef Māris Jansons gathered experience at Riga's top kitchens, Vincents (opposite) and La Bohème (T 6732 1938). He is at the forefront of the 'new Latvian cuisine', combining local ingredients with highly technical methods of preparation. Sommelier Jānis Gailis has assembled an excellent menu from 26 wineries across 12 regions of Italy. The restaurant is housed in a standalone two-storey building beside Vērmanes Garden and has a terrace facing the park. Bibliotēka means 'library', and its interior is themed accordingly – there are bookshelves set on walls, armchairs, oversized anglepoise-style pendant lights, and a bar with sofas custom-made from cushions, and geometric chandeliers.
Tērbatas iela 2, T 2022 5000,
www.restoransbiblioteka.lv

INSIDER'S GUIDE

KAISA KAHU, ART AND FASHION MANAGER

Estonian Kaisa Kahu moved to Riga in 2001 and lives in Torņakalns. 'I love the birdsong, the apple-tree blossom and the wooden houses where old women lean on windowsills. Time seems to stand still, and after rushing around all day in heels, it calms me down.'

On her days off, she'll drop by Innocent Cafe (Blaumaņa iela 34-1a, T 6666 2364) for an 'awesome brunch and coffee', before checking out the art scene, 'remarkable for such a small country', at intimate spaces such as XO (see p028), Alma and Bastejs (see p072). A unique retail experience can be enjoyed on Alberta iela, at the shoe stores Madam Bonbon (No 1-7a, T 2022 2235), in a beautifully furnished art nouveau apartment, and ZoFA Atelier (see p086). She also suggests making an appointment to visit the studios of avant-garde fashion designer Keta Gutmane (T 2933 5609) and op-art painter Ritums Ivanovs (T 2917 1515).

Meeting friends for a night out, Kahu will start at Vīna Studija (see p047), which hosts exhibitions and a chic crowd, before dinner at Ecocatering Telpa (Matīsa iela 8, T 2037 1179), in a charmingly raw setting in an old factory. 'The charismatic chef really knows his organic food. And I love the peeling paint.' She'll end the night in Piens (see p044), which really crystallises the spirit of creative cooperation in Riga right now. 'New initiatives are popping up, ideas are flourishing, and the city is abuzz,' she says.

For full addresses, see Resources.

ARCHITOUR

A GUIDE TO RIGA'S ICONIC BUILDINGS

Riga may be medieval in origin, but its architectural fame is built on art nouveau heritage: the streets are a treasure trove of facades displaying the national romantic style. The city is also known for the timber homes of Ķīpsala (see p068), which survived due to a shortage of housing during the Soviet era. In more recent years, architects have fought hard to raise awareness and preserve these structures, and they are returning to fashion after years of neglect.

The functionalism that characterised the 1920s and 1930s has contributed to the city's vernacular, throwing up gems such as those found on Kokneses prospekts in Mežaparks (see p067), and the 1939 Laima Chocolate Museum (Miera iela 22, T 6615 4777), which was designed by architect Stanislavs Borbals. The two-hour tours are in Latvian but do include tastings (book in advance).

Since independence, almost all of the new builds, renovations and restorations have been the work of an emerging crop of highly talented local architects. The biggest story is that of the National Library (opposite), previously housed in several locations across Riga. It finally moved into its new headquarters 23 years after the US-based Latvian architect Gunārs Birkerts initially submitted his blueprint. On the west bank of the Daugava facing the Old Town, it is an arresting edifice that is known by Rigans as the Castle of Light, and has become a symbol of the city.

For full addresses, see Resources.

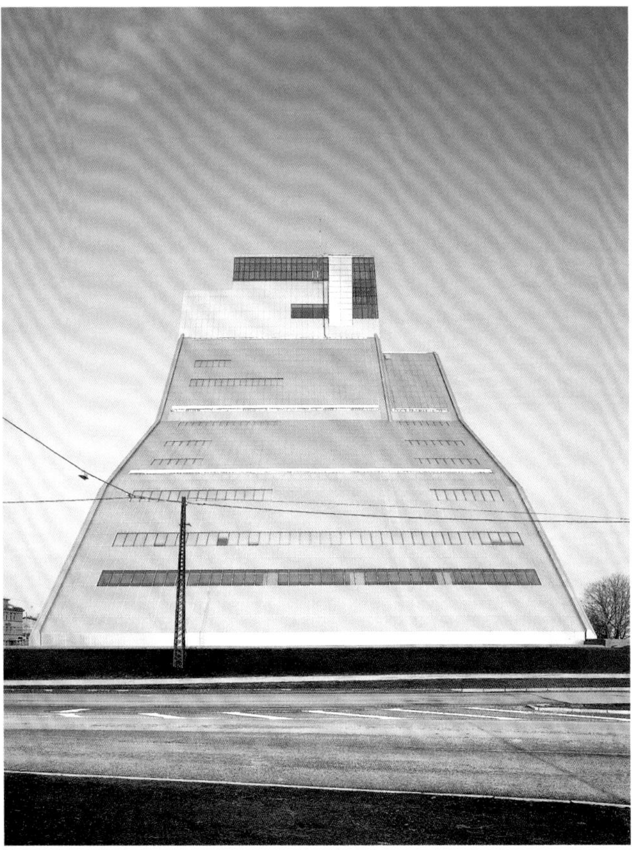

National Library of Latvia

The library's expressive form was inspired by *The Golden Horse*, a story written by one of the country's key figures, Rainis, which tells of a peasant boy scaling a glass mountain to rescue a princess. The tale symbolises the quest for independence, which was regained in 1991, the year that Birkerts finished the design, although it took more than two decades to fund the project. The 13 floors are arranged around a full-height atrium, and the interior colour scheme was gleaned from Lat banknotes, the currency that was replaced by the Euro in 2014. A large proportion of the four-and-a-half-million books and materials were moved on one cold winter's day in 2014, when more than 14,000 people formed a chain and passed them by hand through the Old Town and over Akmens Tilts.
Mūkusalas iela 3, T 6736 5250, www.lnb.lv

National Library of Latvia

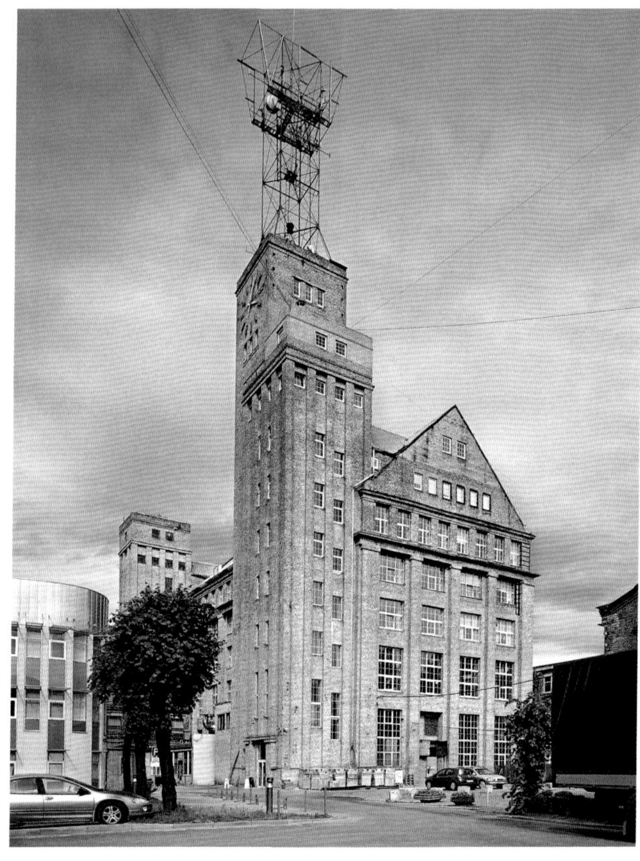

Valsts Elektrotehniskā Fabrika

The State Electrotechnical Factory (Valsts Elektrotehniskā Fabrika or VEF) was one of Latvia's major manufacturing hubs when it was part of the USSR, producing everything from batteries and cars to the famous Minox mini-cameras (see p073). The main building was completed in 1913, and was designed by German architect Peter Behrens, who was a pioneer of industrial classicism. VEF was a Soviet facility during the occupation, before falling into decline. But the past decade has seen it become a hotbed of industry once again, as international companies have moved into the spacious premises. In the nearby VEF Culture Palace (T 6718 1633; open Tuesdays to Thursdays only) there is a 6,000-item museum dedicated to the factory's fascinating history.
Brīvības iela 214

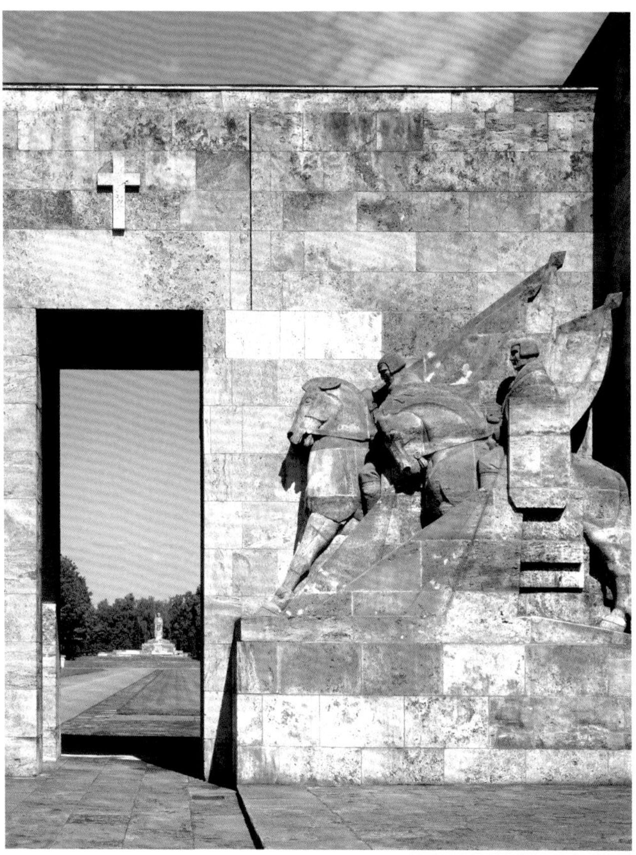

Brothers Cemetery

An impressive example of architecture, sculpture and landscaping working in harmony, the Brothers Cemetery, also known as the Cemetery of the Brethren, the Military Cemetery and the Cemetery of Heroes, honours the Latvian soldiers who were killed in WWI and the country's War of Independence. Built between 1922 and 1936, and designed by sculptor Kārlis Zāle, architects Aleksandrs Birznieks and Pēteris Feders, and landscape designer Andrejs Zeidaks, the cemetery is a nine-hectare park accessed via a monumental concrete gate. An avenue of lime trees leads to the main terrace, where you'll find the eternal flame flickering. Beyond this is the lower-level burial ground, watched over by the travertine statue of Mother Latvia mourning her dead.
Aizsaules iela 1b

Ziemeļblāzma Culture Palace

Lumber magnate Augusts Dombrovskis financed Latvia's first reinforced concrete building for Ziemeļblāzma, the abstinence society. It is thought that Dombrovskis designed it himself, in collaboration with sculptor Gustavs Šķilters, in the prevailing art nouveau style, and it opened in 1913. A reconstruction to mark its centenary, overseen by Juris Skalbergs, recaptured its splendour, and it is now a combination of original elements, like the chandeliers in the main hall, and restored Soviet modifications. In the landscaped French gardens are a replica of Eižens Laube's tea pavilion and an oddly compelling new 35m concrete observation tower (opposite). Today, the palace hosts concerts, theatre performances, festivals and parties.
Ziemeļblāzmas iela 36, T 6784 8849, www.ziemelblazma.riga.lv

Art Academy of Latvia extension

The neo-Gothic 1902 home of Latvijas Mākslas Akadēmijā was designed by Wilhelm Bockslaff as a business school. A master study in brick, its elaborate facade encompasses limestone ashlars and ornamental gables; inside is an art nouveau stained-glass window by Ernst Friedrich Tode and sculptural decoration by August Volz. The desperately needed courtyard extension (pictured) was added in 2012. Architect Andis Sīlis took an existing 1948 red-brick storage block, sunk it by 3m and added glass walls, a concrete access ramp and a cantilevered roof, which, along with the original shell, protects the interior from direct sunlight. The lecture rooms and exhibition halls here are often open to the public.
Kalpaka bulvāris 13, T 6733 2202, www.lma.lv

Day Centre for the Homeless

This unconventional community building is the result of a collaboration between young architectural practices 8AM and Mikus Lejnieks, and provides an inspiring yet low-budget solution to the problem of rising homelessness in Riga. Located in a small plot near the railway embankment, the compact volume is wrapped in tin sheeting, which is cheap, durable and easy to maintain. The sheets are arranged vertically and diagonally, adding visual interest and a certain dynamism to the facade, especially as sunlight refracts and glints off the surface at varying angles throughout the day. By night, the irregularly spaced and differently sized windows, which reveal a warm orange interior, can be seen from afar and help contribute to a welcoming atmosphere.
Katoļu iela 57

Mežaparks

This leafy suburb includes a residential quarter that claims to be one of Europe's original garden cities. The first villas were built in 1902 when the area was known as Kaiserwald, and were laid out according to a plan by German landscape architect Georg Kuphaldt. Over the next 30 years there was a building boom; new houses reflected the art nouveau, functionalist and art deco styles of the era, as well as the elite status of their residents. In the latter half of the 20th century, the district fell into disrepair, but many properties have since been restored and are once again among the country's most desirable real estate. Architecturally interesting streets include Hamburgas, Poruka and Stokholmas. The neighbourhood park has an open-air stage that hosts the climax of the Latvian Song and Dance Festival.

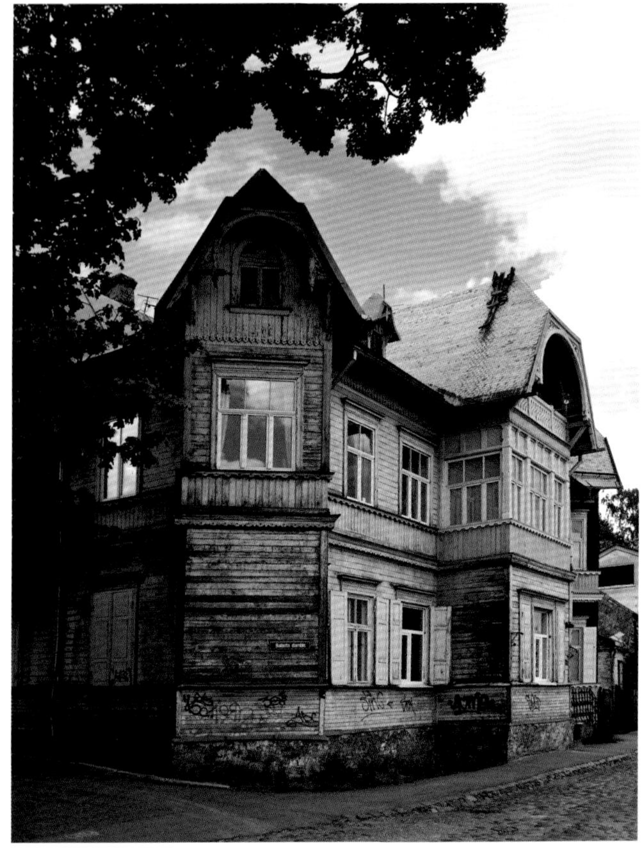

Ķīpsala

In the late 1990s, the island of Ķīpsala was a rambling district of cobbled streets, overgrown gardens and ageing wooden houses, some dating back to the 18th century. A few of these structures remain untouched (above), but most have been carefully restored as part of the area's rapid gentrification. Ķīpsala mainly owes its current popularity to the city's most prolific contemporary architect, Zaiga Gaile, who blazed a trail here with some accomplished renovations of numerous mansions and townhouses, as well as the Ģipša Fabrika loft complex. A converted 1880s plaster factory, it is home to almost 100 swanky apartments, in addition to the delightfully situated Fabrikas Restorāns (see p048). Also in this enclave is the Žanis Lipke Memorial (see p026) and the striking Ķīpsala sports complex (see p094).

Splendid Palace

Often considered to be the most beautiful cinema in Europe, the Splendid Palace is an unusual example of 1920s historicism by Frīdrihs Skujiņš. Rich in rococo and baroque details, the elaborate interior displays sculptural patterns by Rihards Maurs and Jēkabs Legzdiņš, and murals by Hermanis Grīnbergs. Completed in 1923, this was the very first venue in the Baltics to show talking pictures. Now host to various film festivals, it screens movies in Latvian, Polish, German, French and English, and the programme includes cult films and box-office hits. The cinema has been renovated to include state-of-the-art sound-and-vision technology. The adjacent wine bar, Tinto (T 6728 9085), is a nice spot for some post-movie analysis.
Elizabetes iela 61, T 6718 1143,
www.splendidpalace.lv

Daile Theatre

The largest state-owned repertory theatre in Latvia, the original Daile opened in 1920 on Lāčplēša iela. In 1959, its founder, the legendary playwright and director Eduards Smiļģis, organised a competition for the design of a new, more prominent building. It was won by architect Marta Staņa, one of the country's most talented modernists. Completed in 1976, and topped off with a relief by Latvian sculptor Ojārs Feldbergs, the Daile Theatre is a true gem – each of its various spaces have received different architectural treatments. The central auditorium seats 1,000, while there are two smaller theatres and a sedate café. It often puts on foreign plays, some of which are in English. Check out the striking lobby for the symmetrical staircases, concrete pillars and hardwood mezzanine.
Brīvības iela 75, T 6727 0463,
www.dailesteatris.lv

SHOPPING

THE BEST RETAIL THERAPY AND WHAT TO BUY

Historically, Latvia is famous for hand-knitted woollens that come in a kaleidoscope of bright colours and feature geometric designs based on nature, such as suns, stars and fir trees. Check out stores like Tīnes (Riharda Vāgnera iela 5, T 6721 1009) and the carts that pepper Vecrīga. Once prized all over Europe, Laima chocolate was first produced in 1870 and the company now makes more than 250 different products. There are outlets and cafés all over town, but the museum/shop on Miera iela (see p056) is the most interesting.

For one-of-a-kind souvenirs, drop into the ecologically sound Pienene (Kungu iela 7-9, T 6721 0400), stocking wares by Latvian artisans, including Piebalga porcelain and Latgale pottery, drinks such as rhubarb wine, and natural cosmetics from the likes of the Mádara brand, which utilises extracts from Baltic plants. There's also a range of natural beauty products, soaps and bath accessories at Stenders (Galerija Centrs, Audēju iela 16, T 2651 6822), where the attractive wrapping makes for covetable gifts.

There is plenty of contemporary design on show too – stroll down Tērbatas iela to find Riija (see p077) and Paviljons (see p082) before a break at Vīna Studija (see p047). Art collectors should visit the galleries Māksla XO (see p028), Alma (Rūpniecības iela 1-2, T 6732 2311) and Bastejs (Alksnāja iela 7, T 6722 5050), to seek out work by Ritums Ivanovs, Andris Eglītis and Andris Vītoliņš.

For full addresses, see Resources.

Minox spy camera

If you are prepared to scour the markets, you might just find a Minox spy camera. From the 1940s to the 1960s, any spook worth his salt possessed one of these miniature marvels, designed by Latvian Walter Zapp in 1936. They were made by Valsts Elektrotehniskā Fabrika (see p060) between 1938 and 1942, and sported a surprisingly modern-looking stainless-steel body, measuring just 80mm long, perfect for sneaky snaps. Following the war, production resumed in Germany, where the company is still based, but the 17,000 or so models made in Latvia are now difficult to find and highly collectable. The machine's history is documented at the Latvian Museum of Photography (T 6722 2713), whereas the Latgalīte fleamarket (Sadovņikova iela) is an excellent place to start looking for other vintage cameras.

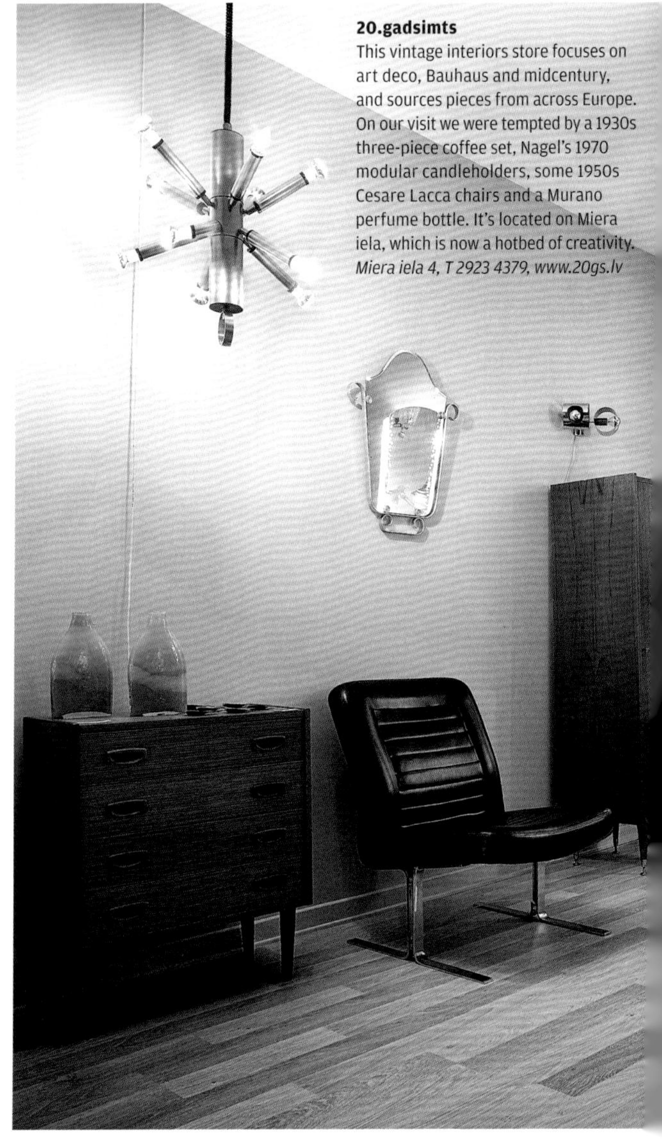

20.gadsimts

This vintage interiors store focuses on art deco, Bauhaus and midcentury, and sources pieces from across Europe. On our visit we were tempted by a 1930s three-piece coffee set, Nagel's 1970 modular candleholders, some 1950s Cesare Lacca chairs and a Murano perfume bottle. It's located on Miera iela, which is now a hotbed of creativity.
Miera iela 4, T 2923 4379, www.20gs.lv

Narciss

Alise Trautmane is a local fashion designer gone global – her London and Moscow outlets opened before this boutique, atelier and café in 2013. The Greek myth informed the look of the store: a large painting of Narcissus by renowned artist Frančeska Kirke conceals the changing rooms, and Rihards Funts has played with the idea of reflection, through mirrors, shiny surfaces and angular furniture like the custom-made counter. Trautmane's ready-to-wear collections are inspired by themes such as folk tales, mythology or polarisation and mix the whimsical with the elegant. She is known for her midi and maxi dresses, but there are also wraps, jumpsuits and coats in natural fabrics like merino, cashmere, silk and lace, plus shoes and accessories. *Bergs Bazaar, Marijas iela 13, T 6728 2785, www.narciss.eu*

Riija

There must be 50 shades of grey within this Latvian lifestyle concept store named after a traditional threshing barn, much of it embodied in a large ecologically sound range of woven linen and wool bedding, loungewear, rugs and towels. These and other wares epitomise design principles rooted in a fusion of rural craftsmanship and modern urban living. More covetable are the original furniture, lighting, pottery and handblown glassware, such as the innovatively coated coloured glass bowls by An&Angel, or the porcelain with dill reliefs by Maira Karstā. Quirkier items include Rijada's apple-tree coat rack, MARA's wooden sunglasses, Mareunrol's leather wallet and the writable T-shirts from Lithuanian brand March Design. *Tērbatas iela 6-8, T 6728 4828, www.riija.lv*

Black Balsam

There's no avoiding Black Balsam when in Riga. It appears in cocktails in every bar. Chefs use it in main courses and desserts, while cafés serve it in coffee or poured over ice cream. The distinctive ceramic bottles emblazoned with black-and-gold labels stare out from countless windows; the miniatures are an easily transportable keepsake. There's even a bar dedicated to the drink – Black Magic (see p040) – in the Old Town. The herbal liqueur is an acquired taste, as it has a slightly bitter, medicinal flavour – as perhaps it should, given how many people rate it as a remedy for everything from digestive problems to flu. A few shots of this 45 per cent ABV tipple and you'll likely feel indestructible too. We're partial to a Black mojito, and on a winter's evening, a Black Balsam with hot blackcurrant juice is rather good.

Putti

Hidden away in a century-old dwelling on a side street, Putti's cutting-edge jewellery and gallery-like concept is a revelation. It presents unique contemporary pieces of exceptional quality from sought-after Latvian makers – Guntis Lauders, Valdis Brože, Andris Lauders, Māris Auniņš, Jānis Vilks – often featuring novel elements and materials like titanium, lava, fossils, mammoth ivory and Roman coins. Iluta Rode's interior combines Macassar wood wall panels and display units, mosaic tiles, spotlighting, black walls with subtle floral detailing, a pair of red 'Ronda' sofas by Wittmann and paintings by contemporary artists Sandra Krastiņa and Roberts Koļcovs. Putti is also the place in which to seek out the conceptual fashion of innovative Riga designers Mareunrol's.
Mārstaļu iela 16, T 6721 4229, www.putti.lv

Central Market

Five former Zeppelin hangars, each 20.5m high and 35m wide, are the unique setting for Riga's Central Market, which opened in 1930. These massive structures are an eclectic mix of art deco, art nouveau and neoclassical elements, and still attract up to 100,000 people every weekday, and close to double that on weekends. This is the place to try Latvian delicacies such as *kvass* (a fermented beverage made from rye bread), pig snouts, birch-tree juice, hemp butter, lightly salted cucumbers, sandthorn marmalade and cheese made with seeds, herbs or dried fruit. You'll also find handicrafts from wood carvings to wicker, ceramics and amber. The retro fish eaterie Siļķītes un Dillītes (T 2961 4012) serves the best sprat sandwich in town, as well as fried eels and Baltic shrimps.
Nēģu iela 7, T 6722 9985, www.rct.lv

p.

Paviljons

Fashion and lifestyle store Paviljons grew out of a 2009 pop-up for young designers and is still going strong. Curated by Elīza Ceske-Feldmane and Agnese Narņicka, it carries a fascinating selection of fledgling and established Latvian labels, as well as pieces from Lithuania and Estonia. Look out for the unisex jeans with witty details by Narņicka's own brand, One Wolf; the asymmetric dresses and art-printed tops by BlankBlank; versatile one-size black dresses by Reinis Ratnieks; QooQoo's vibrant printed leggings, sweatshirts and dresses; and elegant silver jewellery by Anna Fanigina. It's set in a monochrome space given character by the furniture, storage units and decorative items that were recycled from a dressmaking factory. *Tērbatas iela 55, T 2547 4702, www.paviljons.lv*

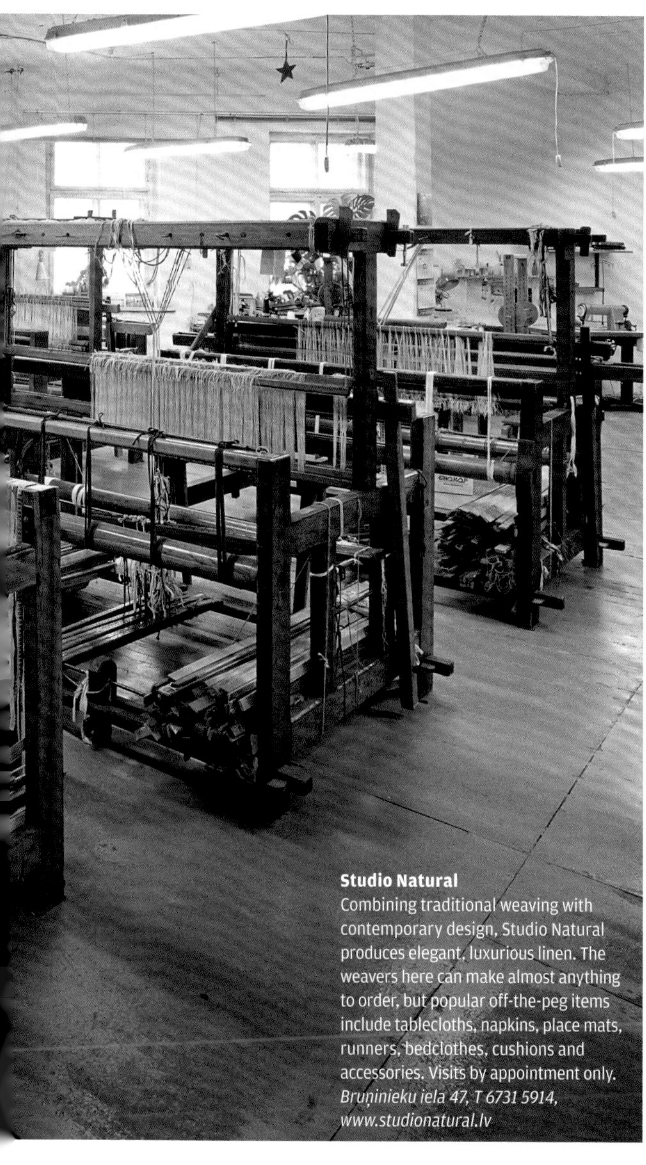

Studio Natural

Combining traditional weaving with contemporary design, Studio Natural produces elegant, luxurious linen. The weavers here can make almost anything to order, but popular off-the-peg items include tablecloths, napkins, place mats, runners, bedclothes, cushions and accessories. Visits by appointment only. *Bruņinieku iela 47, T 6731 5914, www.studionatural.lv*

ZoFA Atelier

Former architect Elīna Dobele says she creates 'houses for our feet', designs that are comfortable and functional but also highly inventive. Handmade locally, the sculptural footwear is a hybrid of strong lines and traditional craftsmanship, as in her calfskin Sharpers Angle Mate (above), €415, which have a folkloric quality. Her Revolvers boots are shown in the Latvian Museum of Decorative Arts and Design. 'I experiment with fabrics and wood to underline the concept of materials as construction elements,' says Dobele, who is branching out into bag and accessory design. Mārcis Šakausks used shoeboxes as the main element in Dobele's playful all-white atelier, ZoFA, where her creations are also displayed behind window and door frames, and on museum-like plinths.
Antonijas iela 22, T 2230 1197, www.zofa.lv

SPORTS AND SPAS

WORK OUT, CHILL OUT OR JUST WATCH

Unlike in many larger cities, the best Riga hotels do not provide the best spas; in fact, most only supply a few bits of gym equipment and a sauna box. One notable exception is the Opera Hotel & Spa (Raiņa bulvāris 33, T 6755 9650), which has an impressive basement facility that includes a Rasul bath – a modern version of an ancient Turkish ritual that uses grades of mud to deep-cleanse and nourish the skin – as well as a striking, cocoon-like mosaic pool. However, you would be better off bypassing the rest of the hotel options and heading to the sleek, Scandinavian-influenced Taka (see p092) or the deluxe six-storey ESPA (opposite) instead.

When the winter chill sets in, it's time for Latvians to visit the *pirts* (sauna). The pastime dates back centuries and practically every village in the country still has a rudimentary bathhouse. For a stylish urban version housed in a bunker, Baltā Pirts (see p093) is the spot. Other cold-weather activities, such as ice hockey, ice skating and under-ice fishing, are very popular. Sigulda, just 45 minutes from Riga, is Latvia's top winter sports centre. The resort even has an artificial bobsleigh run, used by the national team as well as foreign athletes for training and competitions. Experienced skiers and snowboarders will find more excitement at Gaiziņkalns, the country's tallest mountain at 311.6m, and Žagarkalns, which has 14 slopes. Both are about 100km from the capital.

For full addresses, see Resources.

ESPA

This is the first spa complex in the Baltics of such size and splendour, occupying an entire building, a lavish neo-Renaissance gem from 1901, designed by Konstantīns Pēkšēns. The twinkling mosaic interior, a warren of pools, jacuzzis, saunas, steam rooms, experience showers and fitness studios, was conceived by Irish company Douglas Wallace. Highlights are a glass-enclosed heated outdoor pool, and the black-tile spiral stairwell topped by an atrium showcasing Eva Menz's *Morning Dew* – an installation of 2km of metal rope and more than 5,000 crystals that hangs down through all six floors. Try the range of treatments designed for the cold climate that use Baltic amber. The weekend deals encompass a stay at the in-house hotel.
Baznīcas iela 4a, T 6771 5222, www.espariga.lv

Daugavas Sporta Nams

The hotels in Riga are lacking in decent swimming pools, so if you feel like a dip, you'll have to take your trunks to a public one. This modernist concrete complex was designed by Wladimir Schnitnikow in 1962. The first roofed sports facility built in Riga after WWII, it features a highly impressive ribbed vaulted ceiling, put together from prefabricated units, that enshrines a 25m pool with elegant diving platforms, as well as a hall where basketball and five-a-side football is played. A decade previously, Schnitnikow created Daugavas Stadions (Augšiela 1), another concrete multi-use centre that hosts the five-yearly Latvian Song and Dance Festival, which is one of the largest amateur choral events in the world, featuring 30,000 performers.
Krišjāņa Barona iela 107, T 6731 7763, www.basketbolaskola.lv/sport

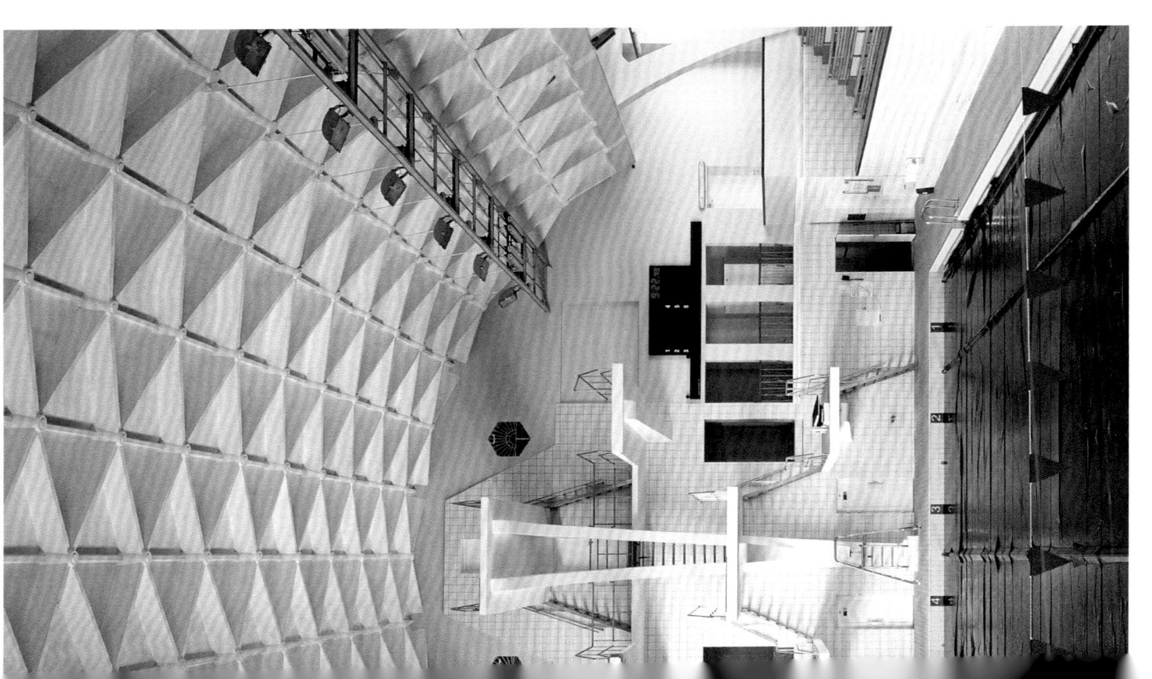

Taka Spa

In 2001, journalist Dina Vjatere and ad executive Agnita Vāvere saw an article on Stockholm's Åhléns Spa in Wallpaper* magazine. Inspired, they decided to set up their own venture and commissioned Swedish architect Mårten Friberg and Latvian interior designer Māris Banders. The result, Taka, opened in 2006 on a tram route overlooking Kronvalda Park. From the moment you enter, there is a serene, tranquil feel here. Three pools of differing temperatures stimulate blood flow and improve circulation, as does the sauna, steam room, and lime, ginger and sea-salt scrub treatments. For the ultimate way to seal a deal, book a business meeting in the yoga/Pilates studio, followed by a relaxation session in the pools and sauna. *Kronvalda bulvāris 3a, T 6732 3150, www.takaspa.lv*

Baltā Pirts

To take a sauna the Latvian way, you build up a sweat, invite someone to beat you with birch, oak, maple and juniper twigs and then plunge into an icy pool – and repeat. Baltā Pirts first opened in 1908, financed by Hugo Lapiņš, who imported coffee to Europe from Nicaragua. At that time, homes only had shared toilets so the bathhouse was an essential part of society, and Baltā served 2,000 people daily until the 1940s. Now run by Lapiņš' great grandson, it is still heated by wood. Choose your weapon (the twig bundles are prepared just before the summer equinox) before venturing into the network of hot and cold rooms. There are separate areas for men and women (Latvians tend to bathe naked). Open Wednesday to Sunday. *Tallinas iela 71, T 6727 1733, www.baltapirts.lv*

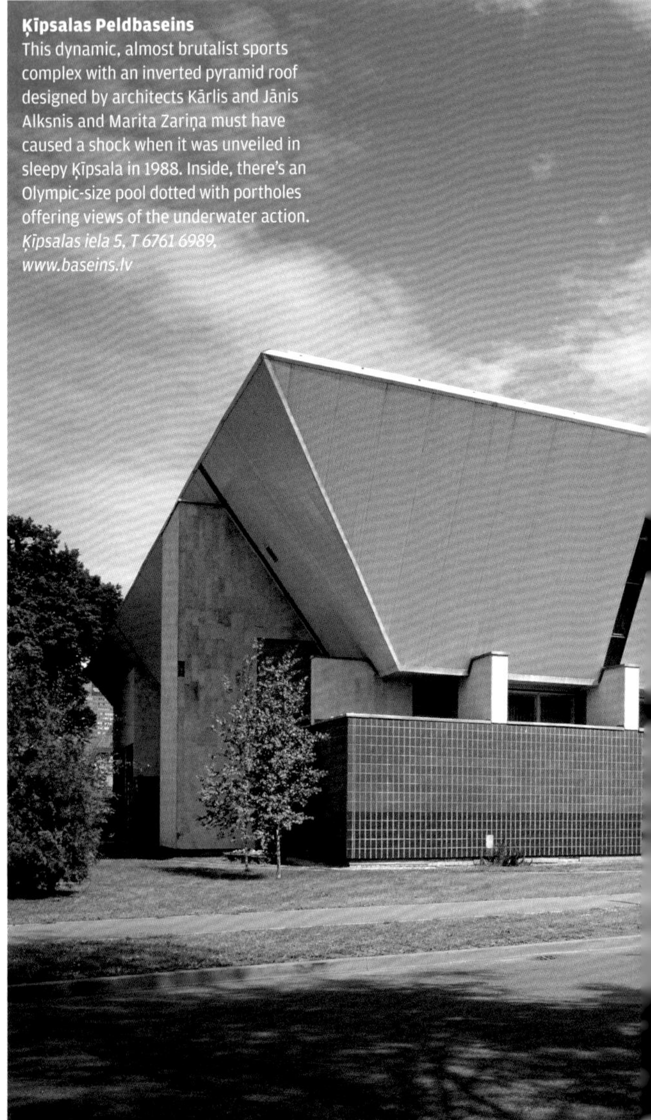

Ķīpsalas Peldbaseins
This dynamic, almost brutalist sports complex with an inverted pyramid roof designed by architects Kārlis and Jānis Alksnis and Marita Zariņa must have caused a shock when it was unveiled in sleepy Ķīpsala in 1988. Inside, there's an Olympic-size pool dotted with portholes offering views of the underwater action.
Ķīpsalas iela 5, T 6761 6989, www.baseins.lv

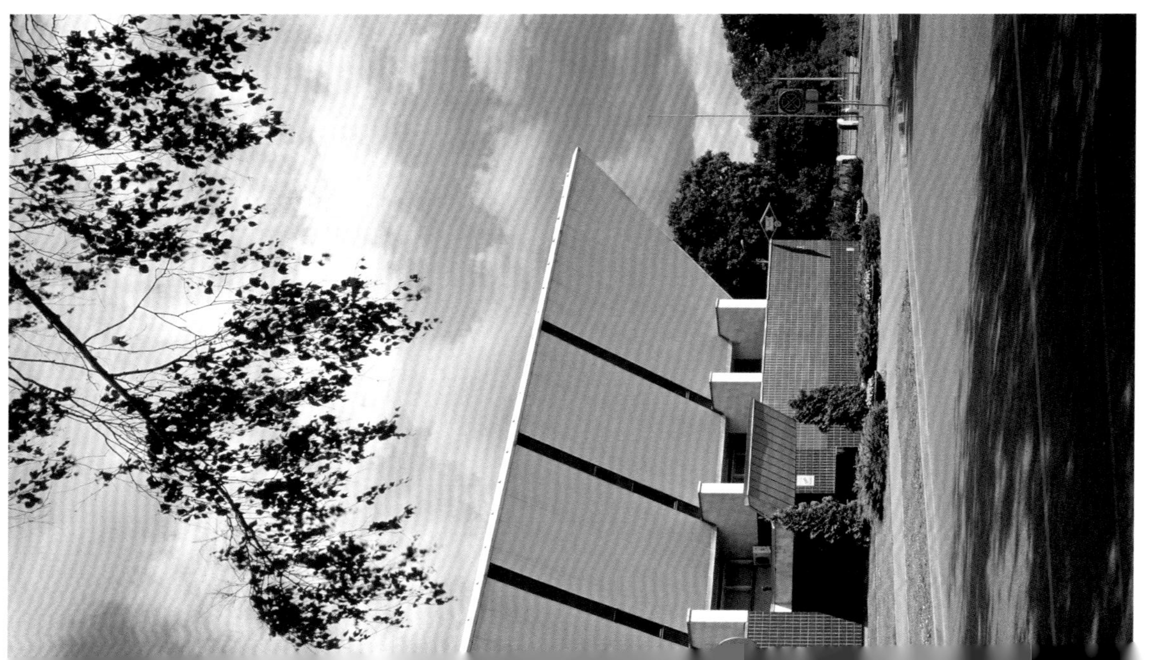

ESCAPES

WHERE TO GO IF YOU WANT TO LEAVE TOWN

Jūrmala is Riga's answer to the Hamptons, full of romantic charm, wooden art nouveau houses and 33km of sandy beaches, all just 20 minutes from the capital. The resort became fashionable with the aristocracy in the 19th century, thanks to its climate, warm waters and medicinal mud, and its numerous spas remain a draw. If you're in a group, rent Villa Morberga (Dzintaru prospekts 52-54, T 2709 9099), a baby-blue 1883 neo-Gothic villa with crenellated towers set in a landscaped park. The Latvian countryside is dotted with impressive palaces and fortresses, such as the fairy tale-like Bauska Castle (Pilskalns, Bauska, T 6392 2280), completed in 1456, and the baroque splendour of nearby Rundāle (see p102). They're some 65km south of Riga. Stop off at the Salaspils Memorial to all those who died in a concentration camp here, an eerie landscape of giant concrete statues. The Abava Valley is known as Latvia's Switzerland because of its forests, flowers and vineyards. Lord it up at Rūmene Manor (see p100), an outpost of Bergs (see p018).

Near the border with Belarus and Lithuania, Daugavpils is the country's second city, and the birthplace of abstract expressionist painter Mark Rothko. A museum (opposite) dedicated to his life and work has been set up in the restored artillery arsenal. Also in the Latgale region is Rezēkne, worth a visit for an outstanding example of contemporary Latvian architecture (see p098).

For full addresses, see Resources.

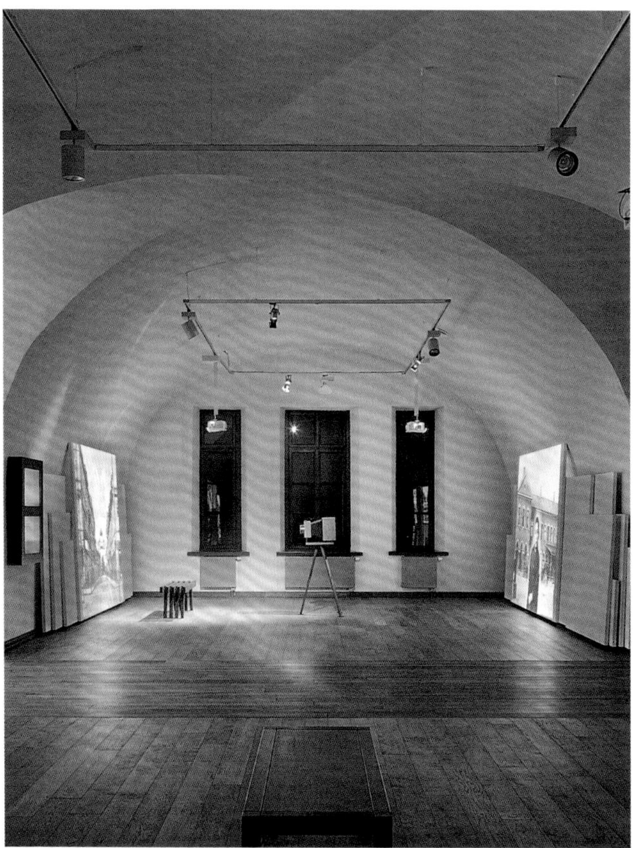

Mark Rothko Art Centre, Daugavpils

It's a little-known fact that Mark Rothko was born in Daugavpils in 1903, to a local pharmacist and Russian mother, his family emigrating to the USA when he was 10. It wasn't until 2013 that the Rothko Centre opened here in the Daugavpils fortress, a splendid example of military architecture, completed in 1833 as a stronghold of the Russian Empire. The collection comprises six paintings and 40 reproductions, the largest body of Rothko's work in Europe. There's also a digital installation set up as if it were Rothko's studio: resting against walls are canvases, on to which his life story is projected. Temporary shows take in contemporary Latvian painting, Russian art or retrospectives on artists of the calibre of Marc Chagall. Closed Mondays. *Mihaila iela 3, T 6543 0273, www.rothkocenter.com*

Zeimuļs Centre, Rezēkne

Architects Saals' ingenious youth centre somehow manages to be both dramatic and unobtrusive. A concrete, glass and wood labyrinth sunk into the ground below a medieval castle mound, its fifth facade is a geometric landscaped roof that forms 87 triangular slopes. Poking through are two slanted towers clad in slate that forms ancient Latvian patterns.
Krasta iela 31, T 6462 2511

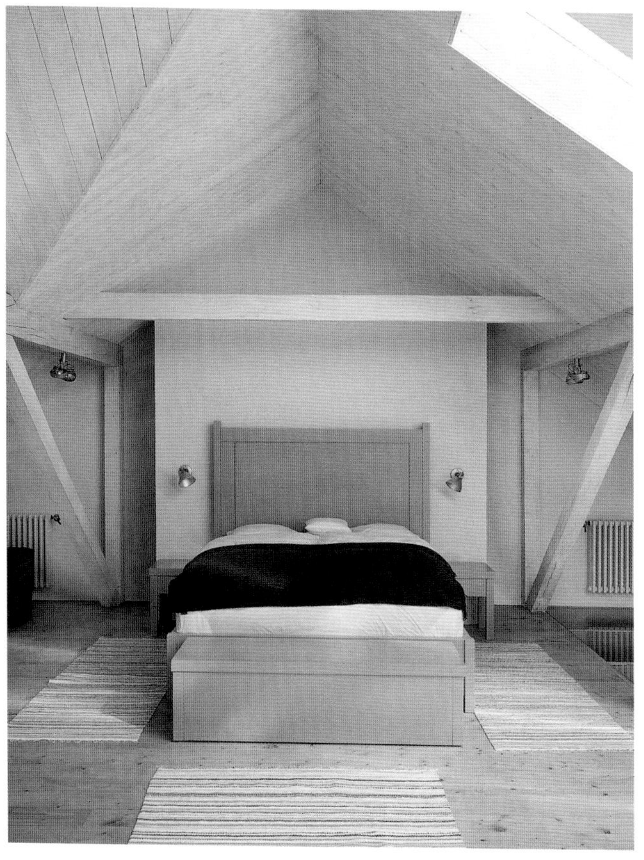

Rūmene Manor, Kandava

Many of the estates of the Baltic-German aristocracy abandoned after Soviet rule are being brought back to life. This 1876 neo-Gothic villa has now been beautifully reinterpreted by Zaiga Gaile as a boutique hotel, using recycled bricks and parquet from other similar houses, reclaimed tile stoves, huge fireplaces, period furniture and chandeliers. The 13 rooms are spread throughout the main building (opposite), The Stable (above) and The Garden House. In the landscaped park by Georg Kuphaldt (see p067), a neo-Renaissance terrace system descends from Rūmene Manor to a lake and island that is accessible via a bridge. Look out for the occasional performances by world-famous Latvian musicians, followed by gourmet dinners courtesy of chef Nauris Jakuško (see p034).
Rūmene, T 6777 0966, www.rumene.lv

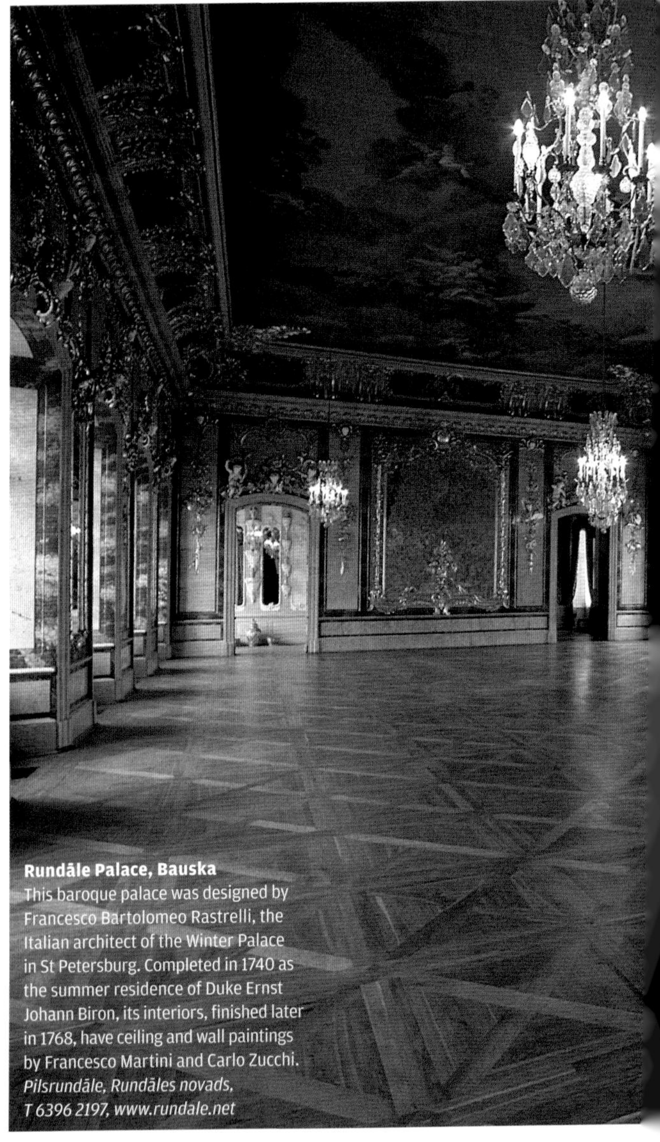

Rundāle Palace, Bauska
This baroque palace was designed by Francesco Bartolomeo Rastrelli, the Italian architect of the Winter Palace in St Petersburg. Completed in 1740 as the summer residence of Duke Ernst Johann Biron, its interiors, finished later in 1768, have ceiling and wall paintings by Francesco Martini and Carlo Zucchi.
Pilsrundāle, Rundāles novads, T 6396 2197, www.rundale.net

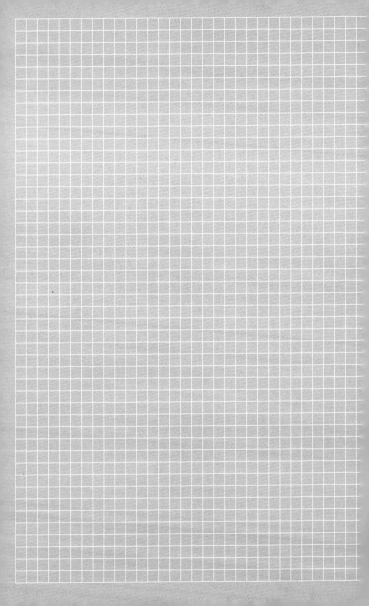

NOTES

SKETCHES AND MEMOS

RESOURCES

CITY GUIDE DIRECTORY

A

Academy of Sciences 015
Akadēmijas laukums 1
T 6722 5361
www.lza.lv

Aleksandrs Vanags Building 024
Krišjāņa Valdemāra iela 69

Alma 072
Rūpniecības iela 1-2
T 6732 2311
www.galerija-alma.lv

Andalūzijas Suns 033
Elizabetes iela 83
T 6728 8418
www.andaluzijassuns.lv

Aqua Luna 024
Andrejostas iela 4
T 6765 0922
www.aqualuna.lv

Arsenāls Exhibition Hall 024
Torņa iela 1
T 6735 7527
www.lnmm.lv/en/arsenals

Art Academy of Latvia Extension 064
Kalpaka bulvāris 13
T 6733 2202
www.lma.lv

Art Museum Riga Bourse 024
Doma laukums 6
T 6722 3434
www.lnmm.lv/en/mmrb

B

Baltā Pirts 093
Tallinas iela 71
T 6727 1733
www.baltapirts.lv

Bastejs 072
Alksnāja iela 7
T 6722 5050
www.bastejs.lv

Bauska Castle 096
Pilskalns
Bauska
T 6392 2280
www.bauskaspils.lv

Bibliotēka No 1 053
Tērbatas iela 2
T 2022 5000
www.restoransbiblioteka.lv

Bistro Priedaine 028
Strēlnieku iela 1a
T 6728 2122
www.bistropriedaine.lv

Black Magic Bar 040
Kaļķu iela 10
T 6722 2877
www.blackmagic.lv

La Bohème 053
Jura Alunāna iela 2
T 6732 1938
www.laboheme.lv

Brothers Cemetery 061
Aizsaules iela 1b

Bufete Gauja 037
Tērbatas iela 56
T 6727 5662
www.bufetegauja.lv

C

Cabo Cafe 046
Annas Sakses 19a/
Roberta Feldmaņa iela 8
T 2863 9556
www.cabo.lv

Central Market 080
Nēģu iela 7
T 6722 9985
www.rct.lv

D

Daile Theatre 070
Brīvības iela 75
T 6727 0463
www.dailesteatris.lv

Daugavas Sporta Nams 090
Krišjāņa Barona iela 107
T 6731 7763
www.basketbolaskola.lv/sport

Daugavas Stadions 090
Augšiela 1
T 2914 1199
www.daugavasstadions.lv

Day Centre for the Homeless 066
Katoļu iela 57

Desa & Co 030
Spīķeri
Maskavas iela 4
T 6721 6186

E

Ecocatering Telpa 054
Matīsa iela 8
T 2037 1179
www.ecocatering.lv

Eižens Laube Buildings 024
Brīvības iela 37, 47, 62

Emils Gustavs 036
Aspazijas bulvāris 21
T 6722 8333
www.gustavsgifts.com

ESPA 089
Baznīcas iela 4a
T 6771 5222
www.espariga.lv

F

Fabrikas Restorāns 048
Balasta dambis 70
T 6787 3804
www.fabrikasrestorans.lv

First Dacha 024
Andrejostas iela 4a
T 2654 0555
www.firstdacha.com

Freedom Monument 012
Brīvības bulvāris

G

Galerija Istaba 042
Krišjāņa Barona iela 31a
T 6728 1141

Garage Wine Bar 033
Elizabetes iela 83-85
T 2662 8833
www.vinabars.lv

I

Innocent Cafe 054
Blaumaņa iela 34-1a
T 6666 2364
www.innocent.lv

J

Janis Rozentāls and Rūdolfs Blaumanis Memorial Museum 024
Alberta iela 12
T 6733 1641
www.memorialiemuzeji.lv

Skyline Bar 050
Radisson Blu Hotel Latvija
Elizabetes iela 55
T 6777 2282
www.skylinebar.lv
Spīķeri 030
Maskavas iela 4
www.spikeri.lv
Splendid Palace 069
Elizabetes iela 61
T 6718 1143
www.splendidpalace.lv
Star Lounge Bar 043
Albert Hotel
Dzirnavu iela 33
T 6714 2749
www.alberthotel.lv
Stenders 072
Galerija Centrs
Audēju iela 16
T 2651 6822
www.stenders-cosmetics.lv
Studio Natural 084
Bruņinieku iela 47
T 6731 5914
www.studionatural.lv
Swedbank Headquarters 013
Balasta dambis 1a
www.swedbank.lv

T

20.gadsimts 074
Miera iela 4
T 2923 4379
www.20gs.lv
Taka Spa 092
Kronvalda bulvāris 3a
T 6732 3150
www.takaspa.lv
Tīnes 072
Riharda Vāgnera iela 5
T 6721 1009
www.tines.lv
Tinto 069
Elizabetes iela 61
T 6728 9085
www.tinto.lv
TV Tower 014
Zaķusalas krastmala 1
T 6710 8643
www.tvtornis.lv

V

Valsts Elektrotehniskā Fabrika 060
Brīvības iela 214
VEF Culture Palace 060
Ropažu iela 2
T 6718 1633
www.vefkp.lv
Vilhelms Ķuze 036
Jēkaba iela 20-22
T 6732 2943
www.kuze.lv
Vīna Studija 047
Stabu iela 30
T 6727 6010
Elizabetes iela 10
T 6728 3205
www.vinastudija.lv
Vincents 052
Elizabetes iela 19
T 6733 2830
www.vincents.lv
Vīnu Veikals 038
Kalnciema iela 35
T 6761 4322
www.kalnciemaiela.lv/vinuveikals

HOTELS

ADDRESSES AND ROOM RATES

Albert Hotel 016
Room rates:
double, from €70
Dzirnavu iela 33
T 6733 1717
www.alberthotel.lv

Hotel Bergs 018
Room rates:
double, from €175;
Penthouse, €350
Elizabetes iela 83-85
T 6777 0900
www.hotelbergs.lv

Hotel Centra 023
Room rates:
double, from €40;
top-floor suite, from €70
Audēju iela 1
T 6722 6441
www.hotelcentra.lv

Dome Hotel 020
Room rates:
double, from €150;
Deluxe Suite 201, from €360
Miesnieku iela 4
T 6750 9010
www.domehotel.lv

Europa Royale 016
Room rates:
double, from €70
Krišjāņa Barona iela 12
T 6707 9444
www.groupeuropa.com

Grand Palace Hotel 022
Room rates:
double, from €190;
Junior Suite 303, from €300
Pils iela 12
T 6704 4000
www.grandpalaceriga.com

Hotel Neiburgs 017
Room rates:
double, from €215;
eaves suite, from €380
Jauniela 25-27
T 6711 5522
www.neiburgs.com

Radisson Blu Hotel Latvija 009
Room rates:
double, from €95
Elizabetes iela 55
T 6777 2222
www.radissonblu.com/latvijahotel-riga

Rūmene Manor 100
Room rates:
The Stable apartment, from €500;
Garden House, from €1,000;
Manor House, from €3,500
Rūmene
Kandava
T 6777 0966
www.rumene.lv

Hotel Valdemārs 016
Room rates:
double, from €65
Krišjāņa Valdemāra iela 23
T 6733 4462
www.valdemars.lv

Villa Morberga 096
Room rates:
prices on request
Dzintaru prospekts 52-54
Jūrmala
T 2709 9099
www.jurasmols.lv

WALLPAPER* CITY GUIDES

Executive Editor
Rachael Moloney

Editor
Jeremy Case

Authors
Evelina Ozola
Agnese Kleina

Art Editor
Eriko Shimazaki
Original Design
Loran Stosskopf
Map Illustrator
Russell Bell

Photography Editor
Elisa Merlo
Assistant Photography Editor
Nabil Butt

Production Controller
Natalia Read

Chief Sub-Editor
Nick Mee
Sub-Editor
Farah Shafiq

Editorial Assistants
Emilee Jane Tombs
Blossom Green

Contributor
Anne Soward

Interns
Ayaka Nakamura
Victoria Purcell
Rosemary Stopher

First published 2009
Revised and updated 2014

All prices are correct at the time of going to press, but are subject to change.

Printed in China

Phaidon Press Limited
Regent's Wharf
All Saints Street
London N1 9PA

Phaidon Press Inc
65 Bleecker Street
New York, NY 10012

www.phaidon.com

A CIP Catalogue record for this book is available from the British Library.

ISBN 978 0 7148 6837 0

PHOTOGRAPHERS

Ingus Bajārs
Zeimuļs Centre, pp098-099

Roger Casas
Riga city view, inside front cover
Hotel Neiburgs, p017
Dome Hotel, p020, p021
Žanna Café, p025
Māksla XO, pp028-029
Kim?, p030
Koya, p031
Garage Wine Bar, p033
Vīnu Veikals, pp038-039
Star Lounge Bar, p043
Piens, pp044-045
Cabo Cafe, p046
Vīna Studija, p047
Bibliotēka No 1, p053
Kaisa Kahu, p055
National Library of Latvia, p057, pp058-059
Ziemeļblāzma Culture Palace, p062, p063
Art Academy of Latvia extension, pp064-065
Day Centre for the Homeless, p066
20.gadsimts, pp074-075
Narciss, p076
Riija, p077
Putti, p079
Paviljons, p082, p083
ZoFA Atelier, p086
ESPA, p089

Hans Georg Roth/Corbis
Rundāle Palace, pp102-103

Antje Quiram
Vanšu Tilts, pp010-011
Freedom Monument, p012
Swedbank Headquarters, p013
TV Tower, p014
Academy of Sciences, p015
Hotel Bergs, pp018-019
Grand Palace Hotel, p022
Hotel Centra, p023
Alberta iela 2a, p027
Restaurant Bergs, pp034-035
Vilhelms Ķuze, p036
Bufete Gauja, p037
Black Magic Bar, pp040-041
Galerija Istaba, p042
Fabrikas Restorāns, pp048-049
Skyline Bar, pp050-051
Vincents, p052
Valsts Elektrotehniskā Fabrika, p060
Brothers Cemetery, p061
Mežaparks, p067
Ķīpsala, p068
Splendid Palace, p069
Daile Theatre, pp070-071
Central Market, pp080-081
Studio Natural, pp084-085
Daugavas Sporta Nams, pp090-091
Taka Spa, p092
Baltā Pirts, p093
Ķīpsalas Peldbaseins, pp094-095

Christoffer Rudquist
Minox spy camera, p073
Black Balsam, p078

Ansis Starks
Žanis Lipke Memorial, p026
Mark Rothko Art Centre, p097
Rūmene Manor, p100, p101

RIGA

A COLOUR-CODED GUIDE TO THE HOT 'HOODS

ĀGENSKALNS
This peaceful quarter is a step back in time, and a newfound retreat for Riga's creatives

ĶĪPSALA
You'll traverse this island on the Vanšu bridge during the short drive in from the airport

MASKAVAS
A former Russian district and Jewish ghetto, Maskavas has plenty of Soviet-era relics

CENTRS
Dine in Riga's most exclusive restaurants among the outstanding art nouveau buildings

VECRĪGA
The museums and array of architecture in this UNESCO World Heritage Site are a delight

ANDREJSALA
North of Centrs, on the river, this abandoned area is showing the shoots of regeneration

For a full description of each neighbourhood, see the Introduction.
Featured venues are colour-coded, according to the district in which they are located.